Eating a Light Bulb

does not make you

Bright

———————

Eating a Light Bulb

does not make you
Bright

Written and Illustrated by

Wendy Hamilton

ZealAus Publishing

Eating a Light Bulb does not make you Bright
Light on Home-schooling

Copyright © 2019 by Wendy Hamilton
Illustrations © 2019 by Wendy Hamilton

www.zealauspublishing.com

All rights reserved. No part of this book may be reproduced or transmitted in any form or by any means without written permission of the author. Some names have been changed to protect the identity of persons

ISBN: 978-1-925888-35-5 (sc)
ISBN: 978-1-925888-09-6 (hc)
ISBN: 978-1-925888-19-5 (e)

Dedicated
to my mother
Shirley
Who lived her life
for her children.

Contents

Introduction 1
Every Man has his Price! 4
A New Direction 10
D Day 14
Breaking the News 18
Binding Up the Mouth 27
Spontaneous Learning 35
Curriculum Programs and Jargon 41
Quilts and ABC's 49
Letterland and the Inflatable Rubber Raft Problem ... 56
Teaching Scripture the Easy Way 60
The Miracle Swirl 65
What About Socialization? 73
A Seminar a Birthday and a Boy 80
The Education Review Office 87
Birthdays and a Wish 94
I Still Want a Horse 101
Praying for a Horse 105
Weeds 114
The Silver Lining 118
Noise Monitoring 126
Purple Pants 135
A Modern Problem? 142
It is a Marathon Not a Sprint 148
Unexpected Blooms 156
Mark 162
More Propaganda 166
Digging for Victory 172
Prologue - University 181
About the Author 183
Other Books By Wendy Hamilton 184

Home Sweet Home.

Wendy Hamilton

Introduction

"I love your house. Where do you buy your furniture?"

The question threw me. I stared at my visitor like a possum caught in the headlights of a car.

"Where did I get my furniture?"

Not at some chain store like she was hoping.

I looked around my lovely farmhouse kitchen. The centerpiece of the timber-lined room was an antique wood stove. It sat in black magnificence under a tall fire-surround and mantelpiece. The wooden kitchen table with ladder-back chairs and rush seats looked right with it. As did the Persian rug on the floor, the rocking chair, and cuckoo clock. Even the cast iron coffee grinder was carefully selected. No slick coffee machine was going to mar the ambiance of my 1922 bungalow.

"I pick them up here and there," I replied lamely thinking of tag sales and junk shops.

The rocking chair was a garage sale bargain.

The grandfather clock, a flea market score.

Eating a Light Bulb does not make you Bright

I won an iron bedstead at an auction and rescued a stool from the dump.

A treadle sewing machine came from a neighbor.

But the braided floor rug flew all the way from the U.S.A, stuffed into my suitcase like an inflatable rubber raft before the string is pulled.

It could take years to find just the right Tiffany lamp for the hall table or whistling kettle for the woodstove.

And acquiring the right piece was just the beginning. Then it had to be cleaned and polished, sanded back, re-upholstered or repaired so that it blended in perfectly. They were all individually crafted pieces not assembly line products because you cannot bung an eclectic mix of modern furniture into a house like mine if you want something special. You do not get this look out of a chain store; just as actors in movies are not wearing off-the-rack clothes. It is impossible to get the superb fit of Hollywood clothes without customization.

It occurs to me most children receive a chain store off-the-rack education. We send our little five-year-old's out of their homes to get their first educational suit of armor. The suit is one size, expected to fit all. It is upgraded every year and takes no account of individual weight, height or shape. No one wonders whether a five-year-old is ready to wear such a heavy suit. If the child is fortunate enough to be born an average height and shape, the suit might not chafe too much. But pity the extremely short, tall or late-blooming child. He will have to adapt as best he can. If his legs are too long, saw his ankles off. If the helmet sticks, bang it on with a hammer.

Now line up all the children born in the same year and expect them to compete in a race. Everyone will be graded against their peers and judged against the standardized 'normal.' The number one child who breaks the tape and rides the slim forefront of the educational bell curve will be honored at the end of the year with prizes. But the little chap still floundering about at the rear is in trouble. His legs are so short the unyielding armor suspends his feet at the kneecaps. He will be in remedial reading and Special Education all his formative years and leave school convinced he stupid.

Would the world have the elegant concept $E=MC^2$ if the retarded dummy Einstein had fitted the standard mold better? The expert teacher who called him an idiot is the one history has branded a fool.

To all you parents who are looking for a more customized education for your children, I say, "it is possible to put together a low-cost education that fits your child like tailored clothes."

It may not look very impressive in the early years, just as a fine painting at a garage sale has little honor. But with love, prayer, and support, your child can cut the cloth of his own learning and mold his education into a perfect fit.

This generation is facing an enormously changing world. When innovation and flexibility are becoming increasingly essential, it makes little sense to hammer kids into ill-fitting rigid suits of armor. After all, the battle of life is no longer fought with lances and horses.

Eating a Light Bulb does not make you Bright

Every Man has his Price!

I was absolutely opposed to home-schooling. There was no way I was going to turn my beautiful 1920s bungalow into an ugly school! Classrooms are horrid. Spelling lists on walls and paper fish dangling from metal rafters make me feel nauseous.

"Forget it!" I said loudly and often.

I would not destroy the ambiance of my 'Little House on the Prairie' bedrooms with posters of the solar system and multiplication tables. Neither would I screw a whiteboard onto the timber walls of my country kitchen, or pin crayon monstrosities on my fridge with alphabet magnets. Subsequently, when our eldest daughter turned four, I enrolled her in preschool and looked forward to a two-hour break every afternoon. It was not, however, the break I thought it would be.

"Hurry up, Marie finish your lunch," I barked. I wiped

Hannah's hands and face before pulling the two-year-old out of her high chair. The pressure of getting anywhere on time with two small kids was stressful. I lifted the stroller off a hook on the back porch and flicked it open.

"I said hurry up Marie!" My irritation and snappiness escalated as the clock's hand inched closer to one pm. I dumped Hannah into the stroller, grabbed Marie's hand, and rushed out the door. It was amazing how preschool dominated my life, I thought bitterly as I arrived at the Kindergarten and lined up with all the other mothers dropping off their kids. My flexible days suddenly had a rigid stake driven through them I had to revolve around.

"One moment Mrs. Hamilton," the head teacher stalled me as I turned to leave, "here is the envelope for this term's compulsory 'donation,' and five books of raffle tickets to sell. We expect every family to support the upgrade of the playground. Also, we are having a bake sale to raise money for more books. What can I put you down for?"

I took the envelope and raffle tickets and mumbled truthfully that I was not much of a cook.

"A cake wonderful, make sure it is hereby nine am Saturday morning. Don't forget we are looking for people to man the stalls and take charge of the bouncy castle. Please support us by being there and telling all your friends to come."

She turned to the woman beside me and handed her an identical envelope and the standard stack of raffle tickets. While her back was turned, I took the opportunity to slink away.

I wonder what sort of books they are intending to buy? I thought. Will they be the benign antics of a hairy dog out for an unaccompanied walk, or stories of children being

Eating a Light Bulb does not make you Bright

eaten by witches? I felt insecure about giving people I did not know a daily blank check of two hours to write whatever ideology they wanted on my child's impressionable mind.

I looked at Marie as she ran off. She had a tendency towards ADHD behavior that spiked as our quiet home was swapped for this supercharged environment of kids, noise, and activity. I watched her briefly. In a space of a few minutes, she rushed from the finger painting to the sandpit, to the giant dolls, to the jumbo blocks, then back to the finger painting. She did not settle at anything. I turned to go home. I could not hang around as I needed to get back for my baby's afternoon sleep. Already she was nodding off. As I passed out of the gate, I glanced back in time to see Marie rush out, scoop a handful of sand into a bucket, throw it down, and run inside again.

At home, I put Hannah in her cot and wound up the musical mobile. The plastic Sesame Street characters revolved slowly, and the tinkling sounds dimmed as I shut the door. I thought I might snatch a quick sleep myself. I set the clock alarm for an hour. But by the time I had a cup of tea and flicked quickly through a magazine, there weren't enough minutes left to make it worthwhile. I left it as long as I could before rousing Hannah. I really hated to wake a sleeping toddler. If she got overtired, she was cranky in the evening and hard to settle at night. As I strapped my daughter (howling because of her interrupted nap) into the stroller, I noticed that it had started to drizzle. Where was the pushchair cover? In the woodshed of course. The last and most unlikely place I thought to look. I gathered up Marie's raincoat and my umbrella and bounced the stroller down the veranda steps.

"I'm late, I'm LATE," I puffed, as I ran down the street.

I had a heart-rending mental image of Marie sitting alone on the steps of the kindergarten feeling abandoned and forgotten. I ran faster. The wheels of the stroller splashed dirty water onto my jeans as I flew across the road. A steady stream of umbrellas, mums, and kids, were pouring out of the gate when I arrived hot and breathless, with my blood pressure alarmingly high. I looked for Marie and was relieved to see that she was not sitting alone on the steps. She trotted towards me clutching a painting.

"What did they teach you today?" I quizzed her as we sloshed home through the rain.

"Stuff."

"What do you mean by stuff?"

"Nothing."

My normally verbose child who drove me crazy with her constant talking was as silent as a clam. It was common for her to express weird ideas. When I was with her twenty-four-seven, I could always think back through the day and decode cryptic comments. The two-hour gap, however, interfered with my ability to stay totally in touch with my child's inner world, and I felt I had lost something very significant.

"I have to pick up some bread before we go home," I said to Marie as I steered her into the supermarket.

"Hello Wendy, I haven't seen you for a while," a friend greeted me. "That's a pretty picture," she said looking at the soggy flower and large yellow sun that my daughter still clutched in her hand. Julie turned her attention back to me. "Did you know that Kay and Jane and Karen have decided to home-school?"

"Yes, and did you know Hannah and Jill are too?"

"It seems like lots of our friends have decided to home-school. What about you Wendy, are you going to?"

Eating a Light Bulb does not make you Bright

"ABSOLUTELY NOT! I hate schools and I would not want to ruin my home by turning it into a classroom," I said shuddering.

"I totally agree. I am against home-schooling because…………"

Julie started listing off reasons while I lapped them up; agreeing with them all.

"Mummy, can we go home now?" Marie tugged at my arm. I glanced at my watch.

"Oh, Julie look at the time. I've got to fly. Ian will beat me home if I don't hurry up. It's been great talking to you."

As I walked off, a pleasant glow enveloped me. It was so nice to talk to someone on the same wavelength. Home-schooling was a hideous idea. I had only got in the door and removed all our wet weather gear when the phone rang. It was my sister.

"Hi, Antoinette," I said.

"What are ya up too?"

"Oh, just the normal old routine, what about you?"

"Nothing much."

"Guess what, I met up with Julie in the supermarket, I haven't seen her for ages and we had a great talk about the evils of home-schooling this afternoon."

"Ooo, fancy home-schooling, I can't think of anything worse."

"No, nor me either, just imagine one of those dental hygiene charts hanging above the bathroom mirror ahh!"

"I agree, so yuck!"

"I don't know why some of my friends are thinking of doing it?"

"They're crazy."

"Yeah, I agree, crazy. However, it would be nice to

have my afternoons back, and I don't like feeling so out of control."

"That's true. You can't be sure what they're teaching nowadays."

"Yeah, and don't forget all the raffle tickets we have to sell and cakes we are expected to bake."

I glanced idly at Marie's picture lying in a soggy heap on the kitchen table as I talked. In the right-hand corner, the name Joan Smith was printed boldly in red marker pen. I had not noticed it before.

"Hang on a minute Antoinette," I said pulling the phone away from my ear.

"Marie come here. Is this your picture?"

"Yes," said Marie, looking me full in the eye.

"Are you sure, did you really paint this?"

It was very strange that a kid who couldn't stick to an activity for more than thirty seconds would stay focused enough to produce a picture.

"Yes," she repeated dropping her eyes, her tongue sliding around the inside of her lips.

"Who is Joan Smith?"

"A girl who hates me,"

"I'm sure she doesn't," I said automatically.

"Yes, she does!" Marie spoke with conviction.

I looked at my daughter, I looked at the stolen picture and experienced a paradigm shift.

"We will talk about this after I get off the phone," I said sternly as I picked up the receiver again.

"You know Antoinette, as much as I hate stuffed fish, multiplication charts, and crayon monstrosities, I hate lack of control, and negative socialization more. Call me crazy if you like, but I have decided to home-school."

Eating a Light Bulb does not make you Bright

A New Direction

"I don't think Kindergarten is doing Marie any good," I said to Ian later that evening during our nightly pillow talk.

"She just rushes around from one activity to another like a hyperactive kangaroo. Today she came home with another kid's picture and lied about it. I have noticed a definite deterioration in her behavior. And the other day I overheard a nasty little girl scream, 'I hate you,' at her. I think she might be Joan Smith, the child Marie stole the picture from."

"Take her out then," said Ian promptly. "It's not compulsory, and if she is getting naughty and bullied, it is not worth it."

"Mmm," I said thoughtfully. "I had an interesting conversation about home-schooling with Antoinette this afternoon. Actually, it was more of a monologue than a conversation. I was telling her how much I hated the idea of home-schooling when I started to list some of the reasons why people might be tempted to go down that track. I was right in the middle of it when I realized Marie had pinched a picture, and all of a sudden I felt convinced I should home-school our kids! I know we have discussed at length how I would go on all the school trips and you would be on every school committee when our kids got to that age, but we have never once talked about the possibility of me home-schooling. I suppose it is because I have been so loudly against it. I am ashamed to admit it, but I can't even guess how you feel about the idea."

"Wendy, if you would home-school our kids it would be a huge relief and one of the greatest gifts you could give me," answered Ian in a heartfelt tone.

"Wow! I never even suspected you felt like that," I said in surprise.

"Nor did I until you suggested it," he smiled.

"I'm not sure how to teach reading," I said doubtfully, "but it must be easier to fix reading problems than drugs, lying, and stealing."

"You'll do fine," said my husband encouragingly. "Marie doesn't have to go to school legally until she is six years old. Just because everyone starts their kids at five doesn't mean they have to. So that gives you two years to practice before you have to do anything. Besides, you're not teaching rocket science! Take Marie out of kindergarten tomorrow."

"You're right and I will," I said with determination.

"Good on you, your turn to switch off the light."

I padded over the floor in my bare feet, flicked off the light and crawled back into bed. Ian beside me dropped off to sleep with wondrous ease. I, however, lay in the dark wishing I could switch off my mind as easily as the electricity.

In my head, I walked all around the Kindergarten, from the outdoor play area to the reading corner. Everything was on a large lavish scale. The sandpit was the size of a school swimming pool. The water play table was bigger than a billiard table. There were four swings, and a rope climbing frame suitable for army training. The dolls were the size of two-year-olds. There were buckets and buckets of blocks and enough soft toys to insulate the wall cavities of a large house. In addition, there was a miniature shop, pretend oven, play dough, finger paint, crayons, and books. When I said everything was on a large scale, I did not include the bathroom arrangement. The ten tiny toilets with little munchkin half doors looked like something out of Goldilocks and the Three Bears.

It was impressive but there was nothing there that I could not duplicate on a diminished scale. Moreover, I could do it without selling raffle tickets cakes or jumps on a bouncy castle. We already had a fenced yard, a tree, and a tire swing. I would buy a giant clamshell paddling pool. I could use the bottom half of the clam as a sandpit and use the lid (on sunny days) for supervised water play. I could get a cheap bucket and spade and borrow expensive water toys from the toy library. I already had pots and pans, spoons and cups, which could be used with sand, water, and play dough. Blocks of all sizes were worth investing in, as were bikes and a trampoline. Christmas was coming. Marie could get a tricycle, and her plastic ride-on scooter could be passed down to Hannah. We already had a lot of books and there was always the library. The more I thought about it, the more it seemed feasible to become my own kindergarten. In reality, a professional teacher did not have magical ability or secret knowledge. A certificate did not make a twenty-year-old girl, fresh out of Teacher's College, better for my children than me. I had a brain, information on child development was plentiful, and no trained professional cared about my children as much as I did.

The big question was, how could I keep my house from looking like a classroom? While it was unimportant to many home-schooling mums, it was important to me. A revolutionary idea hit me. Stuffed paper fish and fridge magnets are not essential for education. I liked where this train of thought was going. The next thought was just as good. Crayon monstrosities, do not inspire budding artists more than prints of Rembrandt and Renoir? Neither do seedlings in a yogurt pot and two tadpoles swimming around a plastic shipwreck, teach more than a cat with kittens in a cottage garden. Furthermore, I have yet to find a nicer way to read a book than snuggled up in a quilt next to a wood fire; especially if the weather is foul.

Suddenly, home-schooling seemed possible.

To take full responsibility for training my children certainly required extra commitment and effort, and I was not sure exactly how to do it. All that mattered was, I knew God was calling me to home-school, and with his help, I could manage it. Moreover, as my husband rightly pointed out, teaching kids is not rocket science!

Eating a Light Bulb does not make you Bright

D Day

I'm going to do it. I'm going to do it. The words in my head kept time with the beat of my feet and the hum of the stroller wheels, as I strode towards the Kindergarten. The raffle ticket books bounced about in my baby-bag. The closed zip hid them from my sight but their presence still irked me. I could not wait to get rid of them and the obligation to make a cake. Those expectations sat on me like a dead weight. They were light, however, compared to the time restriction and the loss of authority. Beside me, Marie trotted unsuspectingly.

"Why are we going to Kindy so early?" she asked confused. "We haven't had lunch yet."

"Oh, I just want to see the teacher about something," I answered vaguely. It was a lovely morning; yesterday's rain had passed off. A bright orange butterfly caught her attention and her question flitted away. At the Kindergarten, I wheeled Hannah into the classroom entrance and tapped on the stroller's brake with my toe.

Wendy Hamilton

A butterfly caught Marie's attention.

Eating a Light Bulb does not make you Bright

"Stay here and watch your sister," I commanded Marie as I zipped open the baby-bag, and gathered up the unsold raffle tickets. The morning class was having 'mat time.' Small children sat clustered around the junior teacher who was reading aloud a picture book. As she turned the brightly colored page, I spied the head teacher in the office.

"Mrs. Banks, can I speak to you for a moment?"

"Yes, what can I do for you?"

The tall woman moved towards me. Her superior height, poise, and age felt intimidating. I pulled courage up from the pit of my stomach.

"I want to give back the raffle tickets, and here is the donation I owe," I said handing her a check. "And," I drew a deep breath, "I have decided to withdraw Marie from the program."

There was a long pause. Mrs. Banks' eyebrows contracted defensively.

"Don't get me wrong, I think you are doing a wonderful job. This is not a complaint. It is just I don't think Marie is emotionally ready to be in an environment with so many other children. She just flits from one activity to another. I think it is better for her to be at home."

"Oh."

The eyebrows relaxed and reformed into patronizing arcs.

"You have nothing to worry about Mrs. Hamilton. We are trained professionals. Your little girl is no more immature than any of the other children. She will be fine."

"Thank you, but I have decided to withdraw her," I repeated.

"But she will be disadvantaged socially and find the adjustment to school so much harder. Besides, you owe it to your community, if you withdraw her we will lose funding."

"I'm sorry but I have decided to home-school her."

"Ohhhhhhh!" There was deep disapproval in the 'oh'. "Well, there is nothing I can do if you are determined to go down this ill-advised track. Thank you for returning the raffle tickets. I assume you will not be making a cake for us this Saturday either?" she sniffed.

"That's right," I mumbled as I sidled towards the door.

"Before you go," (her tone was commanding) "please sign this release form."

I halted reluctantly and scribbled my name on the dotted line, before making my escape.

It was over. I had done it!

As I left the gate and the black iron fence receded, joy and relief flooded my soul and I almost skipped along. The baby bag (stripped of raffle tickets) swung back and forth pleasantly. I hummed a little tune. Oh, happy day, I did not need to stop at the supermarket for eggs and flour because I was not making a cake. On Saturday I would not be serving on the White Elephant stall or taking money for the bouncy castle. They could buy whatever politically correct books they wanted, and Hannah would sleep undisturbed. Best of all, I had been courageous and got my daughter back. And as the stroller wheels spun along the sunny street, my heart sang in time to my feet

"I've got her back. I've got her back!"

And I felt the 'smile' of God.

How quickly and permanently He had changed my reluctant heart. Kindergarten and school may be the way for most families, home-schooling, however, was the right way for us.

Eating a Light Bulb does not make you Bright

Breaking the News

"But I want to go back to kindergarten, I like it!" wailed Marie.

I lifted my daughter onto my knee.

"I know you do Marie, but I don't think it is the best place for you to be. Think about that nasty little girl who said she hates you?"

The smallmouth drooped and there was a thoughtful silence.

"What about the sandpit and the finger paint?" she said at last.

"We can make our own Kindy right here. We can have a sandpit, finger paint, water toys, and all kinds of exciting things."

"Can I have books?"

"Yes."

"And can Bubby play with me in the sandpit?"

"Yes, Hannah can."

"Would I have to see Joan Smith again?"

"No."

"Then I don't want to go back to that old Kindy. I want a new one," said Marie brightly.

"Good girl," I said smiling, as I lifted her off my knee. "Go and find your shoes, we have some shopping to do."

The next morning I felt good as I looked at the result of my shopping trip. There were blocks, crayons, coloring-in-books, seeds, and plasticine. The huge clamshell and little-table-and-chair set were ugly but useful. Unlike the Kindergarten that had lots of activities for Marie to rush around sampling, I decided that one thing each morning was enough. I still needed sand and water-toys for the clamshell, so the girls would not be digging in the sand or playing with water today. Instead, I whisked up a batch of play-dough in my food-processor. It felt warm and pliant in my hands as I worked food coloring through it. So much cheaper than store bought I thought, and much cleaner than the kindergarten stuff that sixty dirty hands fingered and thirty mouths ate, when the teacher's eye was not upon them. I rolled back the floor rug in the kitchen and set the small table and chairs in front of the wood range.

"Here you are girls," I called to Marie and Hannah. "Come and make something."

Four little feet rushed down the hallway, and two small bottoms plunked into the seats. I plopped balls of dough on the table and handed Marie a lumpy cellophane packet. A cardboard slip with the words, 'Little-Miss. Cookie Cutter Set,' fell to the ground unheeded as Marie ripped it open.

"Look at these Bubby," she crowed. "One rolling pin for me and one for you. We can make hearts and circles and………what is this Mum?"

"I think it is supposed to be a butterfly."

Eating a Light Bulb does not make you Bright

My girls sat busily playing with dough.

"Oh yeah, we can make lots of pretty butterflies."

"I'll show you how to roll it out," I said dividing each color into two. "This stuff is Hannah's, and yours is over here, Marie," I said, in the vain hope it would stop fights from arising.

"No don't eat it, Hannah!" I pushed her hand away from her mouth. "It's yucky, very salty, yucky, don't eat it. That's right," I added as she patted and poked at a blue mound.

Marie started to squish her dough balls together.

"Try to keep the colors separate," I said intervening, "otherwise they will turn into a horrible brown. Keep the stuff you are not using in this ice cream container so it won't dry out," I added, putting an empty one in front of her. "Roll it thin like this, now press a cutter into it, then pull all the outside dough away and there you have a…… butterfly!" I ended triumphantly, as I dropped a flat shape onto the palm of my hand.

"Ohhhhhh that's pretty let me make one!" said Marie in excitement.

There was a knock on the front door.

"Here you are," I said giving her the cookie cutter. "Hannah make me some hearts. Marie come and get me if Bubby starts eating it," I called over my shoulder as I went down the hallway and opened the door.

"Hello, Mum and Dad, lovely to see you. Come in and see my kindergarten," I said ushering them in. "I have decided to take Marie out of Mairtown Kindergarten."

"Out of Mairtown?" said Mum in surprise as she followed me down the hallway. "But that is such a good Kindergarten. I have such fond memories of taking Rubella there, strapped to a little seat behind me on my push bike. Why would you do that?"

Eating a Light Bulb does not make you Bright

"I don't think it has been good for her. She was rushing around getting more and more wound up. Look at her now," I said, poking my head around the kitchen door and pointing at her. The two girls sat busily rolling and cutting, too absorbed in their activity to notice us peeping at them. "And Hannah can have her full afternoon sleep now. Going out every day was tiring and disruptive."

"But kindergarten is such good preparation for school," said Mum, unconvinced

"I'm going to home-school," I said, dropping the bombshell.

"I don't think that's wise. You should send them to school," reacted my father. "There are reasons for children starting school at age five."

"No there aren't," I said, walking into the lounge so we could sit down. "I have been doing some research on it. Children used to begin school at nine. The starting age has been slowly creeping down over the years. When I started school, the legal age was seven," I continued, "and even now, I don't have to have an exemption for Marie until she is six. Yet kids go to school at five, whether they showing signs of readiness or not."

I paused and listened to the escalating noise in the kitchen. The busy hum of engaged play had deteriorated into giggling and table thumping. There was no screaming or fighting, however, so I carried on talking to Mum and Dad.

I have been reading the findings of a thirty-year study by Dorothy and Raymond Moore[1]. Their studies show most kids are not ready for formal education until eight or nine

---

[1] Better Late Than Early: A New Approach to Your Child's Education by Raymond S. Moore Dennis R. Moore Dorothy N. Moore 1989 by Reader's Digest Association

years of age, and some boys are not ready to begin reading until they are eleven? The school entry age keeps dropping because it is convenient for the parents, and there is money and jobs in it for teachers.

"Twelve seems very late to begin reading," said my father looking unconvinced.

"You didn't read until you were twelve," I reminded him. "And then you taught yourself by reading the bible."

"That is true" agreed Dad. "School was a terrible place," he added, a faraway look in his eye as he remembered back to the 1940s.

"Grandma told me that she would take you to school and when she arrived home, there you were, sitting on the step waiting for her."

"Yes, I took a shortcut over the fields and ran all the way home," admitted Dad sheepishly. "I got caned every day because I couldn't spell. But schools are not like that anymore."

"That's true," I agreed, "but I still think small children are better at home. I heard yesterday that the New Zealand Government has allocated more funding for early childhood education and some groups are lobbying to make formal education compulsory for four-year-old's."

The giggling in the kitchen turned into squealing and fighting. I slid open the servery hatch between the two rooms and poked my head through.

"Stop that horrible noise and come and say hello to Grandma and Granddad," I said sternly.

"Grandma," shouted Marie.

"Gan-dad," shouted Hannah.

They rushed down the hallway into the room waving lumps of play dough.

Eating a Light Bulb does not make you Bright

"Look at my butterfly," said Marie running up to Dad.

"I made a ball," said Hannah, handing Mum a chewed looking circle.

"Aren't you girls clever," said Mum.

"That's a good butterfly," said Dad.

I pulled a big basket of jumbo blocks into the middle of the room.

"When you girls have finished saying hello to Grandma and Granddad, you can play quietly with the blocks.

I turned back to my parents. "I have also been reading up on brain development," I said, as Marie started building a tall tower. "The best way to get a genius is to give children lots of time to explore, easy access to caring adults, and limited exposure to children outside the family; the complete opposite of the school environment. Then there is the whole bullying issue, don't get me started on that!"

My father cleared his throat and held out his hand automatically for the block Hannah thrust at him.

"I think you should put Marie into school when she is five, and see if you have a bullying problem before taking such a radical step."

"Yes that's right," agreed my mother. "Why not choose a good Christian school? This home-schooling idea is silly, too much work for you, Dear. I loved my time at home alone while all you kids were at school. The holidays were terrible. I hated having you all underfoot again. Besides you're not a trained teacher."

"As tempting as that sounds Mum, I don't think that is the best for my children. And you don't have to be college trained to do a good job. Mothers teach their children how to speak. You don't have to be a trained teacher to get toddlers talking. If all babies for the last hundred years, however, had been put in language schools five days a week, everybody would think a mother couldn't teach her children to speak."

"Oh well, it's up to you I guess," said Mum doubtfully.

"Would you like a cup of tea?" I asked changing the subject.

Later that evening, I told Ian how my day had gone.

"The play dough was successful, but my parents dropped in this morning, and they are not very pleased about our decision to home-school. They think it is a silly idea."

"Oh well, at least they are not the type to interfere and cause trouble over it," said my husband. "Anyone who does something unusual can expect disapproval."

"Yeah, Dad went on about five being an age carefully picked for a reason. He said it like he had solid evidence for his statement, but the reality is, he only said it because five is the status quo, and he has never thought about it or checked out the facts. I told them some of the things Dorothy and Raymond Moore said in their book Better Late Than Early, but they still think we should put Marie into school. Dad says we should wait and see if we have a problem first."

"To be fair on him home-schooling is a new idea," said Ian.

"Yeah, your right. I know they are negative just because it is not normal. Nevertheless, it shook me a little bit. I re-read Better Late Than Early again after they went. I felt I needed the encouragement. I like how the Moore's advocate a balanced mix of study, manual work, and home, or community service. They have lots of teaching suggestions that are very manageable."

"What kind of things?" asked Ian.

"Singing, playing oral games, and identifying the kid's interests, like bugs, and gardening."

Eating a Light Bulb does not make you Bright

"That sounds easy enough."

"Yeah. They also advocate limiting young children's reading to twenty minutes at a time, because longer periods can damage their eyes."

"That's a different attitude," said Ian. "Parents and teachers usually push for early reading."

"Yeah, even many homeschoolers don't take this approach, they are more likely to create a mini-school in their home, complete with workbooks, charts and paper fish on the piano," I said, shuddering.

"You have got a phobia about fish haven't you," teased Ian. "Whenever we talk about school you start going on about fish. You don't like paper fish, fish tanks, or even ceramic fish in the bathroom, and yet you are a fish yourself."

"What do you mean I am a fish?"

"You're a salmon. While all the other fish like to swim in schools, you like to swim against the tide and find your own way upstream."

He was annoyingly right.

"Have a yummy cake," I laughed, handing him a purple blob of play-dough.

Wendy Hamilton

Binding Up the Mouth

Marie's incessant yapping followed me around as I humped ladders and planks about.

"What are you doing Mum, what are you doing? Please, can I help? What color is the sky? Can a centipede walk if one of his legs is broken?"

The ceaseless drivel and questions were doing my head in, and if I did not get relief, soon I would not have the energy for the big project of painting the house. Daily exposure to my first born had taught me that decision making was a finite commodity. I could use it on what color to paint the trim around the window, or answer centipede questions. More than once I have heard the statement, 'there is no such thing as a stupid question.' A scathing "huh," is all I can say to that! Anyone who believes that, has never encountered a kid like Marie. She asked me endless silly questions, like what color is the grass? And why does a fire engine go to a burning house? She already knew the answers, she only asked them to gain my attention. I thought nervously of the mornings she had reduced me to a zombie mentality by nine o'clock. I had less than half an hour to act if I wanted to keep my momentum.

"Yes, you girls can help," I said, as an inspired thought hit me. I went into the kitchen and dug around in the rubbish bin. Good, the empty honey pots were still there. A quick wash and a bit of improvising with wire, and suddenly I had two miniature paint buckets. A further rummaging about in the garage produced two old brushes. They were the small variety for cutting in around window panes. Although they were worn and the bristles starting to fall out, they were still flexible enough to feel real.

"You girls can paint the house," I said filling their buckets with 'paint' from the outside tap. "Come and I will show you how."

They followed me excitedly around to the front.

"Now start up here and move your brush back and forth like this, and work down. Don't stuff it right into the bottom Hannah, just put the tip in. That's right."

The water darkened the red-brown shingles of the bow-window.

"Look, you missed some. Make sure you get it all."

I felt clever as I trotted off to get the real stuff. I would work on the right side of the house, far enough away to be left in peace, but close enough to keep an eye on them.

It worked a treat.

After a little while, I noticed the girls were doing something rather odd. They would paint for a bit then step backward, close one eye, and hold their brush out an arm's length away.

Wendy Hamilton

"Look what I drew, Mum."

Eating a Light Bulb does not make you Bright

What were they doing?

The little mimics! I realized that was exactly what I was doing as I debated whether the green trim around the window was an improvement or not. After a while, they tired of it and Marie was at me again with a barrage of stupid questions.

"That is it, Marie! I want you in your bedroom now." I threw my brush down and stomped inside. "Here are some paper and colored pencils, draw something. I don't want to hear or see you until lunchtime!" I shut her firmly in her bedroom and went back to my painting.

At four-years-old, I had expected some sort of attempt at scribbling long ago, but Marie had done nothing; not even on the wallpaper. A library book on my bedside table charted the specific stages to expect in a child's mental development. The first stage of drawing (the book assured me) is a wobbly circle with blobs for eyes and a slit mouth. Then stick arms and legs protrude from the face and eventually a blob for the body. Small details like hands fingers and toes were much further down the development track. I had little hope of seeing anything as coherent as a circle come from Marie, but I didn't care. Anything to buy a reprieve! For an hour or so I painted undisturbed. I wished I had thought of imprisoning her months ago.

Suddenly, the bedroom window flew open. A perky little head popped out. I groaned inwardly and got ready to blast her.

"Look what I drew Mum." She thrust a picture through the window.

I looked and was amazed. The stinging rebuke for disobeying my command died on my lips. The A4 piece of paper had a real drawing on it! There was a hairy head, with two eyes, a nose, a big smile, and two bright red cheeks. The body (with its abdomen and thorax) looked faintly like a bumble-bee, which the pink and yellow stripes accentuated. The legs and arms were in the right places, as were the feet, hands, and ten fingers and toes. Paint dripped from my brush onto the path but in my excitement, I did not notice. So much for the brain development book! My daughter's brain certainly had its own way of doing things.

"Marie that is so good I can hardly believe it!"

I put my paintbrush down and wiped my hands on a rag.

"Let's stick it on the fridge so everyone can see it."

Marie beamed. The refrigerator was sacred ground; sticking things on it was normally a no-no.

"Can my picture stay there for the rest of my life?"

"No, just for today," I said firmly.

The next morning was business as usual. The front of the fridge was bare again as I painted and Marie yapped. I was tempted to send her straight to her room, but I restrained myself. It was only ten in the morning. I could not have her living in her room all day like Rapunzel.

"Go and play in the sandpit with Hannah," I said snappily. "If you don't stop talking, I will stick your mouth shut with tape."

A big smile lit up Marie's face, and I realized my silly threat had backfired. Of course, she would love the idea. This was the kid who loved to have her face tickled with the feather duster, and her hair sucked up the vacuum cleaner.

"Can I? That would be fun." She bounced around my paint tin driving me crazy.

"Oh alright, but only this once. Go and get me the masking tape."

She rushed off, still talking. In the snippet of silence,

Eating a Light Bulb does not make you Bright

I continued painting the house. I heard her returning long before I saw her. She was still talking. She always talked; even if there was nobody in the room. She handed me the masking tape. I ripped off a generous piece and held it in the air.

"You won't try this on the cat will you?" I asked, thinking of his reaction when she sucked his tail up the vacuum cleaner.

She shook her head.

"And you are not to tape Hannah's mouth up, you understand?"

She nodded.

In between the head shaking and nodding were many words that I did my best to tune out.

"Alright," I said sticking the tape across her mouth.

Oh, the bliss I thought, as she skipped away to show Hannah. She was still making noise but at least the words were muffled and moving towards the sandpit. By lunchtime, the tape had fallen off, and the mouth, making up for lost time, talked nonstop through sandwiches.

"You girls stay in the kitchen until you have finished eating," I said as I left the room. "I don't want you carting food through the house." As I headed down the hall, I could hear the shrill little voice rabbiting on and on. I stopped in the entrance way and hunted through the sideboard for the colored pencils and paper. A cassette-player shoved in the back caught my eye, and I had an inspiration. Marie loved stories. She listened to them without making a peep. Listening to a story or sleeping were the only times she shut up. I pulled it out, along with a box of story tapes. I set the paper and pencils on the small table in her room and inserted a tape into the player. In the kitchen, Marie's endless talking was deteriorating into silly giggling and Hannah was starting to squeal.

"Go and wash your hands," I said to Marie as I stomped back into the kitchen. Then you can go into your room and draw me another beautiful picture like you did yesterday. If it is good enough, it can go on the fridge again," I added, forcing a bright tone into my voice. "You can listen to a story tape while you draw."

"Can I listen to more than one story?"

"You certainly can. I will leave the box of stories in your room and you can listen to as many as you like."

"Goody," shouted Marie rushing off.

"You are not to come out until I say you can," I shouted after her.

I heard the bathroom tap running as she washed her hands, and then the thumping of her feet as she rushed down the hallway and into her bedroom. I wearily wiped Hannah's hands and face and carried her into the back bedroom for her afternoon sleep. Then I made myself a cup of tea. As I sank onto the couch, I could hear the deep tone of the storyteller wafting through the lounge door. It was a pleasant change to the shrill jabbering. I must do this more often, I thought.

From that day on, I shut Marie in her bedroom every afternoon for two hours. Back then I did it through self-preservation. I had to carve out some downtime. I did not anticipate its long term benefit.

"Mum, if you hadn't shut me in my bedroom, I would never have become an author and book illustrator," Marie told me twenty years later. "I would have just followed you around talking for the sake of it. Talking to you was so much fun."

I looked with satisfaction at her charming children's

books. Little mice wearing Victorian clothes floated over the pages in hot air balloons and had adventures in underground tunnels. Their homes in the middle of hollow trees were filled with things from our home. I recognized the grandfather clock, the braided rugs on the floor, and the borders on the walls. I thought of the scripture, 'God turns everything to good for those who love him.' How true, even the soil of a mother's irritation and irate impatience, can produce deliciously good fruit.

Wendy Hamilton

Spontaneous Learning

"I wonder where I put my big vase?"

I bent over and peered into a low cupboard. I should have found the vase before I cut the flowers I thought, straightening up again. I put the arum lilies gently into the sink and covered their sliced ends with water. All through my garden long tapering buds waved on the end of tall stems. I loved spring and the first flowers were extra special. After the dismal wetness of winter, it was delightful to see the lavender, daffodils, and lilies, pop up. I turned back to the cupboard and searched properly. I found all sorts of useless cooking gizmos but no vase.

Perhaps I had put it in the attic.

I walked through to the sun-room. I wish those kids would put the manhole cover back, I thought, gazing at the yawning black hole in the corner of the ceiling. At least they had pulled the ladder up and out of the way.

I uncoiled the rope around the brass cleat on the wall and dropped the bottom of the ladder to the floor. The pulley screeched and the hinges that pinned the top of the ladder firmly to the wall wobbled.

I must tighten those screws and oil the pulley, I thought as I climbed. The round wooden rungs bit into the arches of my feet as I paused at the top, and popped my head through the open hatch.

Daylight from the manhole trickled into the roof cavity for a short distance. Beyond was blackness.

"Can someone turn on the light for the attic?" I shouted. "I forgot to."

There was a sound of running feet and the light snapped on as Marie flicked the switch below me. I looked around in annoyance as I climbed through the hole. The makeshift floor was covered with a mountain of books.

"Why can't you kids leave the books in the bookcase?" I bawled down through the hatch. I knew it was a waste of time because Marie had gone, but I yelled anyway. It relieved my frustration.

I considered calling both girls up to tidy the books away but the temptation to do it myself won. It was so much quicker without them. Usually, I tried to avoid that attitude because it was my job to train them no matter how inconvenient. I decided, however, to let it slip just this once. Methodically I picked up books and whacked them back on the shelves. A box of photographs sat on top of a pile of books. I lifted it off and smiled at the book of colors under it. I remembered 'reading' it to Marie when she was a baby.

"Red block, red ball red poppy."

Turn the page.

"Yellow hat, yellow dress, yellow ball…"

Like everyone else, I only taught colors to my first child. I did not have time to teach red and blue, to Baby-Two, three, and four. Yet they all learned about color without anyone teaching them. I thought of the fuss we had the other day because Hannah got a yellow jellybean instead of a green one. She certainly did not need the book. I put it aside for the Salvation Army Opportunity Shop. It was a boring book not worth keeping. Some new mother, however, would want it for her first chick.

I found it pleasant sitting in the attic. The noise of the kids jumping on the trampoline filtered through the slatted vent at the apex of the gable. A musty smell of roses and lavender wafted down from the dried flowers hanging from the rafters. Above them, the corrugated iron roof rolled away into the darkness as it outran the light bulb's reach. Not all the attic had flooring. The bricks of the chimney rose up through a sea of pink insulation. Among the flotsam and jetsam lurked a foam couch, a couple of easy chairs, and a spinning wheel. On wet days it was a lovely place to be. On top of the bookcase opposite me, I suddenly spied my big vase.

"There you are," I said pouncing upon a large jug. As I lifted it down, a box caught my eye. Golden letters on the lid proclaimed PAPER DOLLS. I drew it off the top of the bookcase carefully. I had forgotten all about this. Above the words was a picture of an elaborately dressed Harlequin in rich colors. I opened the box and lifted out the four cardboard dolls. They were still in pristine condition. I popped a dress on the doll called Lucinda, and let childhood memories roll. The girls were too young for these. They would only wreck them. I put Lucinda back into the box and hid it. When the girls were nine and ten, I would let them have them. The paper dolls had given me an idea, however. I caught up the big jug and lowered myself through the entrance hole;

pulling the ceiling-lid over my head before descending the ladder.

Back in the kitchen, I placed my flowers in the large Victorian water pitcher. The big arrangement was for the front entranceway. I carried it down the hallway and set it on top of the oak sideboard. The cream flowers with their yellow stamens looked beautiful against the dark panels. I slid open the middle draw of the sideboard and took out a wad of paper and a small pair of scissors. Through the open door, I could see Marie climbing a tree in the front garden.

"Come inside Marie," I called. "I have something for you."

"Is it cake?" she asked hopefully as she bounced up the steps and followed me into the kitchen.

"No, it is not morning tea yet. I'm going to show you how to make something. Watch what I'm doing." I sat down at the table and folded a piece of paper into a fan. "See how I fold the paper back and forth like this. Now we draw a doll." I drew an outline on the front fold.

"Watch carefully where I cut." I snipped around everything but the fingers and toes.

"Now see what happens when I pull it open... Surprise!" I said, pulling out a string of paper dolls holding hands.

"Can I make one?" shouted Marie jumping up and down in excitement.

"Of course," I said. She stopped jumping and fiddled with the scissors as I made another fan and drew another outline.

"No don't use that hand you're not left-handed," I said handing her the paper. Marie swapped the scissors around.

Wendy Hamilton

It was pleasant in the attic.

Eating a Light Bulb does not make you Bright

"No, put your thumb through the little hole and your fingers through the big one."

"Like this?" asked Marie.

"That's right, but hold it more upright……..no not like that…...maybe the paper is too thick for you? Here try cutting one layer……...no, not like that, that won't work!"

My irritation was rising. I looked at my daughter's glazy eyes. She did not have a clue how to use scissors. Opening and shutting her hand systematically was beyond her. Once again, I seriously wondered if the child was brain damaged.

"Let's just forget it," I said taking the scissors off her.

"Can I have the dolls you made? asked Marie cheerfully.

"Yes," I said wearily, "and I will make some more for Hannah."

A few weeks later, I happened to need a hammer. As I walked down the back path to the tool shed, I glanced over at Marie. She was sitting on the grass under the grapefruit tree cutting away merrily. The blades of the little scissors flashed as they chopped through layers of paper. Chains of dolls were scattered about under the tree. I leaned against the sun-drenched garage wall and watched in astonishment. It would appear that cutting paper (like color recognition and many other skills) happens spontaneously when a child is ready.

Wendy Hamilton

Curriculum Programs and Jargon

I cruised around the vast array of educational material spread out on tables at the home-schooling seminar. There was a lot to choose from because although the New Zealand law stipulated our children were taught, as 'well as and as regularly as the schools,' how we accomplished that was up to us.

A dark-haired woman stood beside me fingering a popular program.

"My kids do fifty-six pages of schoolwork every day," she said proudly.

I picked up a workbook and flicked through the pages. The contents made me feel sick with boredom. How could she possibly stomach fifty-six pages of this daily? I felt depressed just looking at it. Workbooks with lots of little bitty boxes to fill in irked me. It was like painting by numbers instead of sloshing about with paint on a blank canvas. I remembered the dreadful S.R.A reading program of my youth. I doubt that S.R.A stood for Short, Revolting, and Affected although it should have.

Unlike Little House on the Prairie, the skimpy little S.R.A. stories (printed on the front and back of a color-coded card) had no ability to transport me to another world. In addition, when I finished the final sentence of a Little-House-Book, there were no trite questions about the color of Laura's cow or the name of the dog, as there always were at the end of an S.R.A story.

I dropped the book back onto the table and bought a spelling game, hoping it might accomplish a miracle. When I got home, I knew it would not.

"What you need Wendy is a curriculum, not a program," said my sister-in-law when I shared my frustrations with her. Robyn was a gifted teacher and very helpful.

"A curriculum deals with the philosophy behind education in broad brush strokes of principles and goals. Why don't you send for the New Zealand School Curriculum? It is free and you are eligible to receive it."

"Hmmmm, broad brush strokes," that sounded much more like me. If I were a seafaring woman (which I am not) I would rather sail in a yacht with a compass than fit into the scheduled program of a cruise ship.

I sent for the curriculum, and in due course, a thick wad of information arrived in the mailbox.

I read each page, absorbed it, and reduced it down to its main points. Often complicated jargon boiled down to teaching something simple; like counting from one to twenty or the sounds of the alphabet. Once I distilled the ideas down to bare bones, I divided them into things that happened naturally and things that did not. Anything that could be learned without effort (like color recognition) I ignored. I focused entirely on things that would not happen spontaneously like the ABC's. It was hard work sifting through the wordy document but I persisted.

One morning, however, I needed a break.

"Come on kids," I said throwing the New Zealand Curriculum into a beach-bag. Let's go to the beach. The day is too lovely to spend stuck inside."

I packed a picnic and loaded the van with togs, and towels, sunscreen, water wings, and the million other things that an outing with children required. It took some time to get ready, but at least I did not have to plan it months in advance, hire a bus, or sign any legal forms.

"Go back and get your plastic sandals, Marie," I said as buckled Hannah into her booster seat. There may be sharp oyster shells in the rock pools. You don't want your feet cut."

Marie turned and started meandering back to the house.

"Hurry up, I want to get going!" I yelled at her impatiently as I slid behind the steering wheel.

Finally, we were on the road. I hummed to myself as the wheels spun along. We had not gone far before Marie piped up.

"Are we nearly there yet?"

"Nearly," I said sighing. The beach was six miles away. She would ask that question every bend in the road.

"Let's sing a song," I said brightly. "A…B…C…D…E…F…G" I started singing.

"H…I…J…K…LMNOP" Marie joined in.

"Q…R…S……T…U…V……W…X…Y and Z, now I know my ABC's next time won't you sing with…"

"ME," shouted Hannah loudly, finishing with the only thing she could remember.

Eating a Light Bulb does not make you Bright

A day at the beach.

The beach I chose to stop at was a small indent in a long harbor. The water was shallow and safe with a wide strip of white sand. Moreover, there was a swing set, seesaw and a shady pohutukawa tree that spread its low-hanging branches out invitingly.

I stretched open a stripy deck chair and plonked myself down with The New Zealand Curriculum. As the girls made sandcastles and dug for cockles, and pipis, I decoded the chapter on Exploring our Environment. I found to my joy that many things we just did for fun (like camping, beach trips, museums, and art galleries) were considered a legitimate education.

"I'm hungry," Marie interrupted my train of thought as she dropped her bucket of shells down beside me. "Is it lunch time yet?"

"Oh my, yes it is," I said glancing at my watch. I put down my reading, hoisted myself out of the deckchair, and opened up the back of the van. "Spread this blanket under the tree," I said to her. "Don't take your hat off Hannah, you can carry the apples. Put them on the blanket." I handed her a small bag as I hauled out the picnic basket.

"Can we go for a swim?" asked Marie as we munched sandwiches and ate fruit.

"Not until your lunch settles down," I said. "You can get your feet wet but you're not to swim until I'm with you."

"All right, can I go and play now? she asked wiping her mouth with the back of her hand."

"Have you had enough to eat?"

"Yes."

"Off you go then."

I put the remaining food back in the hamper, slumped back into the deck-chair, and continued reading. As I read, I

Eating a Light Bulb does not make you Bright

wrote small words in a notebook while the girls, a little way off, drew large letters in the sand.

"Can we go for a swim now?" asked Marie running up with Hannah trailing behind.

"Yes, now is a good time."

I helped them into their togs in the shelter of the van.

"Put these on," I said blowing up the water-wings. And wait for me," I yelled at Marie as she started to run off.

She slowed up and waited as I scooped my dress to one side and held it above my knees with one hand. With the other hand, I held onto Hannah tightly.

"Look at me I can float," said Marie as we waded into the water.

"Very good. You try Hannah, sit down. That's right," I said as her feet shot out from under her. I grabbed the straps of her togs and floated her about. She looked surprised, but she did not cry. Marie started kicking her feet and the water frothed up around them. I let them stay in the water as long as I could stand it.

"Time to get out," I said lifting Hannah onto her feet. "You are getting cold."

"No, I'm not," said Marie through purple lips.

"Yes you are, time to get out now," I said firmly, as I pulled Hannah out of the water and wrapped a towel around her.

For the rest of the afternoon, they channeled the incoming tide into dams and pools. When they tired of that, they climbed the tree above my head. Eventually, it was time to go home. I picked up the dripping water-wings, and soggy towels, and packed them back into the van. As I buckled Hannah into her booster seat, Marie's shrill little voice piped up.

"Can we get some lollies on the way home?"

Suddenly I was very tired.

"No, you can't have any lollies." I snapped irritably. "The sugar in candy rots your teeth. If you fill up on rubbish you won't eat the vegetables that your body needs for it to grow strong! Don't fiddle with your seat belt," I added in exasperation, "it needs to be on properly. If we have a crash, it could save your life."

I slammed the side door shut, climbed into the driver's seat, and slid The Prince and the Pauper into the CD player. The wonderful story filled the van as we drove along. The mellow voice of the reader was soothing and I relaxed. Hannah, lulled by the sound, nodded off in her seat. Even better, Marie did not ask me if we were nearly home; not even once.

It had been a great day. I went to bed feeling happy until the twilight zone between sleep and alertness. That was when guilt rocketed in.

Another whole day gone and nothing to show for it. The thought haunted me nightly. What would I show the Educational Review Office if I was called on to justify 'as well as and as regularly as,' when all we had done was go to the beach? The weather was so lovely, and we lived in such spectacular scenery, it seemed a shame to stay indoors. I thought over the day's activities. Instead of making marks in workbooks, the kids had swum in the waves, made sandcastles, found crabs, and small fish in rock pools, dug dams, played on the swings, climbed a tree, written large letters in the sand, counted shells, and divided the cockles from the pipis.

I pinged awake as a thought hit me. The difference between a mother and a teacher is wording. Perhaps I should

Eating a Light Bulb does not make you Bright

reverse the decoding system I used on the New Zealand Curriculum. Instead of simplifying phrases I could turn ordinary language into educational jargon. I slid out of bed quietly so I would not wake Ian, and padded into the lounge. I flicked on a table lamp and grabbed a pencil and paper. Thoughts came quickly and I scribbled them down hastily.

"Listen to what we did yesterday," I said to Ian at breakfast. I pulled out my nocturnal notes and read aloud.

"I took the children to explore the environment. Educational outcomes of the day's activities included,

Physical Education (encouraged large muscle development and coordination skills, with swimming running climbing and swinging.)

Science (Observed marine life in its natural habitat.)

Math (Counted and grouped objects into sets.)

English (Letter formation, and recognition, and exposure to classical literature.)

"Health and Safety (Nutrition, water, and road safety.)"

"Wow you were busy," said my husband impressed, "I thought you just took the kids to the beach because the weather was so good."

"I did. My new language fooled even you. It takes too long writing it like this, however. I think I need a simple quick system for recording the day's activities or I will not keep it up. Some sort of workbook with little bitty boxes that do not require much thinking. Of all the workbooks available I have not seen one like that. Mmmmmm, I've just had a great idea."

The next day I bought a column cashbook for both children. At the top of each column, I wrote, Reading, or Handwriting, Science, Math, History, Music, Art, Crafts, Physical Education, social studies, Technology, or Exploring our Environment. It was astonishing how many of the boxes I could fill in at the end of a day we had done 'nothing,' provided I thought in educational jargon.

I still had the nightly guilt sessions, even with my new system, but they were greatly reduced. Moreover, as proof that I was teaching 'as regularly and well,' my column cashbooks were better than money in the bank!

Eating a Light Bulb does not make you Bright

Quilts and ABC's

I sighed. I needed to stop piecing quilts and do a bit of schooling with the girls. The idea of ABC's was not appealing. I would much rather continue sewing. Time was getting short. I wanted to finish a quilt each for the girls before my baby arrived. I pushed my sewing machine to the end of the table to make room for schoolbooks.

"Come inside girls, it's time to practice your letters," I called out the window. They stopped jumping on the trampoline and trooped reluctantly into the kitchen. I picked up a flashcard of an apple with a large upper and lowercase A on it.

"What sound does apple start with?"

The girls looked at me blankly. We had been over and over this, but as usual, nothing seemed to register.

"What sound does apple start with?" I repeated. "Come on, think about it!...What can you hear at the beginning of apple?"

More blank stares.

"Listen ."
"P," said Marie disinterestedly.
"NO! ah ah ah ah ah pple."
I my temper rose as the frustration escalated. They were obviously as thick as a brick. I swallowed my irritation with difficulty.
"Sit down and do some handwriting."
They meandered over to the table and sat down.
"Hold your pencil like this."
"No, not that hand, you are not left-handed! Hold the pencil like I showed you!"
I prized Marie's contorted fingers off the pencil and repositioned them.
"Now let's see a nice long row of capital ayes and another one of little ayes." I cupped my hand around my daughter's small hand and guided the pencil up, down, and across to form the letter A.
"Right, now you try while I help Hannah."
I looked at the clock. We had been at it for ten minutes but it felt like hours. I felt energy draining from my body at an alarming rate. Worse still, the horrible curtain of malaise was dropping over my mind as it usually did when I tried to teach. Why was it I could quilt for six hours and feel energized at the end of the time? Yet I was exhausted after ten minutes of teaching my kids?
I positioned Hannah's fingers and went through the same futile exercise. As the line of ayes progressed slowly and sloppily, I glanced over at Marie.
"Stop playing with the cat," I said waddling over and confiscating him. "You are supposed to be writing the letter A. Turn your feet around and sit on the chair properly." I put the cat outside and shut the door. "Now get on with it before

Eating a Light Bulb does not make you Bright

I get very cross."

I watched over her shoulder for several minutes before turning back to Hannah. She had stopped writing and was chewing bits off the eraser.

"Yucky, spit that out Hannah," I said mechanically. I repositioned her fingers on her pencil. "Up, down, and across. Up, down, and across. Now you try," I said letting go of her hand.

I looked over at Marie once more. As I expected, she had stopped again. She sat slumped in her chair. Even with her back shaped like a banana and her chin level with the table top, her feet dangled. She looked as bored as I felt. Suddenly, I could not stand another minute of it.

"Get down!" I said in exasperation. "School is finished for the day. If you play nicely, I will read you a story after lunch."

"Yay," they shouted rushing off.

I staggered into the lounge and dropped onto the couch wearily. There was a home-schooling support group on tonight. I wanted to go, but I felt such a fraud. Not much schooling was going on in our house. There would not be any counting today. And yesterday, when we did do counting, there was no reading.

I thought of all the mothers who dropped their kids off at Primary School every morning and felt jealous. I wanted to hand the responsibility of educating my children onto another person.

I would love to have them out of the house for five hours a day. Only the deep conviction God wanted me to mold and train their characters myself kept me at the thankless task. What troubled me the most was that I who was diligent and conscientious, just could not get it together!

Wendy Hamilton

"Hold the pencil like I showed you"

Eating a Light Bulb does not make you Bright

That evening my sense of failure deepened as I sat at the support group. I looked around all the other women and wished I had not come. I bet they were doing a better job of teaching their children than I was. After a cup of tea and introductions, the meeting started.

"I want to welcome everyone here and thank them for coming out tonight," said the hostess. "I thought we could go around the circle and share what is happening in each of our homes."

Inwardly I cringed. Perhaps I could gloss over the really bad bits and play up the few successes.

I tensed, as one by one the woman told about their children's progress and the programs and books they found helpful. For a brief moment, I wished I had signed up for the A.C.E. program that was commonly used. It would be nice to say we did X amount of workbook pages a day. But who was I kidding? We would not have managed any pages.

Finally, there were just two women left; myself and Violet Blast. While the other ladies were strangers, I knew Violet from way back. We had lost touch but tonight our circles collided.

She took the center stage with a flourish. A competitive woman, she knew she could win hands down. Her two children were very close in age to mine.

"I get my housework done, and then I sit down and just enjooooooooooy my children!"

Her rich melodious voice filled the room. She lingered over the word enjoy and drew it out to an abnormal length so we could all feel her delight over being the mother of such delicious little ones.

"Last week we did a unit study on bread."

Violet unfolded a beautifully presented portfolio of the

history and manufacture of bread. I looked at the lovely neat handwriting and compared it to the mess my girls had produced this morning.

We had not even started putting C A T together. This, however, was all properly spelled. And the artwork! There was no way Marie could have drawn an ear of wheat like that.

Along with all the other women in the room, I felt myself deflating as the presentation progressed. I much preferred the sanguine little Vietnamese lady, who said she unschooled from a horizontal position, and picked her plumber on the basis that he would let her kids help him. While I felt for the plumber (he must have been desperate for work) she made me feel better about myself. At least I was trying to do something.

Violet Blast finished on a triumphant note and sat down. What could anyone say after that! I looked around the quiet overawed room. Violet had her victory, but at what cost?

It was my turn to speak. It occurred to me I could give a gift to these flattened women.

"Well, I am still struggling to teach my kids their ABC's and keep myself from strangling them!" I said succinctly.

There was a laugh of relief as the tension of inadequacy broke. Nobody would go home feeling even remotely as good at mothering or schooling as Violet, but at least they could feel they were doing a better job than me.

The next day, I was too exhausted to even pretend to home-school. As I revitalized by sewing hundreds of little squares together, I pondered on Violet's portfolio.

Suddenly, the obvious hit me. Even if Violet's children were geniuses, there was no way a five and six-year-old drew and wrote all that.

Eating a Light Bulb does not make you Bright

Violet must have done it herself!

I laughed. Of course, it was Violet's work! Why hadn't I realized it immediately? Well, if she wanted to spend her time putting together unit studies about bread, good on her.

I had more pleasant things to do. I was making beautiful quilts to hand down the generations. In two hundred years her portfolio on bread would not be in a museum. My quilts, however, just might be.

Wendy Hamilton

Letterland and the Inflatable Rubber Raft Problem

Apparently, I am a small person. People tell me I am. I find it hard to believe as size is relative. I am five foot two in the morning and five foot nothing in the evening. All my baby books have charts showing growth lines lower than average. This suggests I grew up to be small. My sister, however, is four foot eleven and my mother four foot nine with size-one feet; which (in my family) makes me a tall, big-foot.

The second reason I have trouble feeling small is my overabundance of stories and opinions. I try to keep them under wraps but given an audience, they automatically inflate like an invisible rubber raft, until the whole room is smothered by them. I realize the entire restaurant has been listening only at the end of the story. They couldn't help

Eating a Light Bulb does not make you Bright

themselves. Not because I am so eloquent or riveting but because I have inherited the family VOICE that deaf old ladies love. Moreover, my volume increases if there is an audience. It is not conscious, it just happens.

The VOICE is proof that my inside is bigger than my outside.

I find most people are gracious about this idiosyncrasy. There is one, however, who is not. I am married to him. Unfortunately, he comes fully equipped with a competing rubber raft. We find each other fascinating when we are alone. But when we go out together, ahhhhhhhhhhh! As we walk into a room two gigantic rafts inflate BOOM and collide horribly.

We would get along better if we had the same style. A story or opinion from me will take twenty minutes; complete with body and facial movements. The same story from him (unfortunately he knows them all) can be done in three. It is so annoying to have someone blurt out the crunch line just as you are setting the scene for your opening line. It is like snipping the head off a long-awaited Christmas Lilly the day before it blooms. But what can you expect from a man who did the Denver Museum in twenty minutes? As nobody wants to hear the full story after they have heard the crunch line, I come off worst in the competition. I have to content myself with smiling graciously while I kick him under the table. It has taken us a while to learn how to manage our unwieldy rubber rafts. We have come up with the old divide-and-conquer rule. He gets half the room and I take the other half. This way we stay friends. Sometimes we have a little talk before we go out.

"Now tomorrow night Wend, try to remember nobody is going to be interested in Letterland. I know you have been struggling over the whole reading issue but this is a Christmas party and none of the guys in the limestone quarry are interested that Bouncing Ben goes bh in words!"

I knew he was right, but it was going to be hard to keep this glorious find under wraps.

It was my wonderful sister-in-law who first introduced me to Letterland. She was a bit of a rubber raft herself and was telling everyone of her find.

"It's an English program," she told me excitedly. "It is used in half the schools in Britain. Its power is every letter becomes a character and the sounds are linked to pictures and stories."

"Hmmmmmmmm," as a right brained person myself, that idea appealed to me. I sent for Lyn Wendon's books First Steps in Letterland[2] and Big Strides in Letterland, plus a set of flashcards and awaited the post with anticipation.

I had bought a lot of flashcards and programs in the past but they had all turned out a disappointment. This one, however, was different. I found myself learning. The school ditty of 'I after E except after C' always left me puzzled. I still had no idea what it meant. And why do S and H change their normal sounds when they stand together? Letterland had the answer. Naturally, silence-loving Hairy-Hat-Man objected to a hissing snake beside him.

"So don't expect Hairy Hat Man and Sammy Snake to be saying their normal sssss hih sounds when they stand together in a word because Hairy Hat man turns around and tells Sammy to Shhhhhhhh!" I read out loud.

The kids and I looked at each other in satisfaction. The logic was watertight and the flashcard showing the H silencing the S memorable. Phonics were no longer a

2   www.letterland.com.au

hideous chore. Marie even badgered me for Letterland stories. There were vowel men who dabbled in ice-creams and oranges. Despicable robbers who stole elephants and ink, while witches poisoned apples to make them taste AWFUL. Personally, I didn't go for the witch bit, so my kids knew her as the Wicked Wild Woman instead. I found my own spelling improving and the septic spelling scab that festered all through my school years lost some of its sting.

I was excited about my find. Nightly pillow talks became an equal mix of cement chemistry and vowel stealing robbers as Ian and I talked about our day. All went along swimmingly until the night before the Christmas party.

"You won't tell the blokes about Letterland, will you?" he repeated nervously. "None of the guys in the limestone quarry are interested that Bouncing Ben goes bh in words!"
"Of course not" I assured him. "I only tell women with children about it."

"Well, I know you!" said my husband darkly. "You might plan to keep it under wraps, but before we know it, you will be on a roll and half the restaurant will know that Clever Cat goes kh in words!"

I sighed. He knew me too well.

"Just promise me you will not talk to my boss or the General Manager."

"It's a deal!" I said. "I will only talk to the women married to the men in the bagging plant. And I will sit as far back in the corner as possible."

"Well that will have to do," conceded my husband. "I am glad Christmas parties only happen once a year. Just one more thing, try to keep your voice down. Sometimes it is hard to remember you are only a small woman. I doubt I could lose you in a football stadium!"

Wendy Hamilton

Teaching Scripture the Easy Way

The end of the day, oh blessed relief. The kids were bathed prayed over and in bed. Everyone was fed and nobody was dead. Anything more was a bonus. Four kids had ground me down to realistic expectations. I loved my new definition of success. It brought the bar down low enough to win.

On the hall table sat a cassette player. I pushed the play button and a rich, cultured voice filled our home.

"Then the Lord said to Moses go to Pharaoh and say to him this is what the Lord says: Let my people go so that they may worship me. If you refuse to let them go, I will plague your whole country with frogs………"

The kids lay in bed listening. We did not have the drink-of-water fiasco in our household thanks to Bible on cassette. They all loved lying in the dark listening to the Bible as they dropped off to sleep. Ian and I also enjoyed listening. Evenings were nice; especially nice for me. I got a quiet

Eating a Light Bulb does not make you Bright

house and Ian all to myself. I treasured those evening hours. All too soon it would be dawn again. When the automatic timer clicked the cassette on at 6am, the battle between Moses and Pharaoh would continue.

The next morning I stumbled about cooking breakfast as Moses unleashed locusts, blood, and flies upon the Egyptians. Ian smelling eggs wandered into the kitchen and put his Bible on the table.

Oh no I thought. He is going to have another shot at family devotions. I felt guilty at the thought. The motivation to pass on our faith was admirable. The reality, however, was painful. This morning was like every other time. The children and I sat around the table listening to Ian as he read a passage of scripture.

"Marie you can read the next verse," he said at length.

"Palm twenty-three," read Marie.

"Not palm, Psalm, the P is silent," instructed Ian.

"Psalm twenty-three……….. The Lord is my sh sh,"

"Put your finger under it and sound it out," I said encouragingly.

"Shep shep…… sheep head?" said Marie hopefully.

"No, shepherd."

"Oh, shepherd……….. I shall not be in want, he makes me lie dh oh ww nn."

"No Marie, you pronounce o and w as ow it's he makes me lie down," I sighed wearily.

One little verse read by an amateur reader was like a thick rubber band; it stretched a very long and tiresome distance. The toddler grizzled and banged his spoon in boredom. He had my sympathy. Like Mark, I could not wait to be finished and released with a prayer. I looked forward to the inevitable day when morning devotions would quietly slide out of our lives. It would take us six months to notice their disappearance.

Eventually, the agony was finished.

"Try and do a little bible memorization today," suggested Ian as he kissed me and left for work.

Later I gathered the children around.

"Now who can say the memory verse? We read it this morning after breakfast."

Four blank stares.

"Come on, Psalm twenty-three. I'll help you with the first part to get you started. The Lord is my………..what?

"Friend?" said Marie hopefully.

"Well yes he is, but that's not it. The Lord is my shhhh?"

"Shell!"

"Don't be silly, how can he be a shell? Think about it, we have been over this many times," I said, feeling beaten.

There was a long pause. The fog of defeat descended like a numbing cloud over my mind. It did not matter whether it was times tables or bible verses, the end result was always the same; extremely disheartening.

"The word is shepherd……. I shall not be in want," I said in an unsaintly tone.

"What doesn't he want?" asked Hannah.

"King David is not saying he doesn't want things, he is saying he will have everything he needs."

"Why doesn't he just say it that way?"

"Because he wants to say it this other way," I replied irritably.

"Can we go and play outside?" asked Joe.

"Yes, that is a good idea," I agreed with relief. I felt I needed a strong cup of coffee. Three minutes of that sort of interaction with my kids totally unraveled me. It was so uncomfortable and forced. I much preferred answering questions as we walked along the road. Questions about the pretty butterfly in the hedge, or where the cat went when he died.

It was a small step from wings to intelligent design, a little hop from cat-heaven to life after death.

As I sat in the lounge and sipped my coffee, I could hear the kids playing outside. Marie's shrill little voice floated through the window.

"I'll be God and Moses. Hannah, you be Aaron, and Joe can be Pharaoh. Here you will need a stick," she added as she handed Hannah a broom. "You stand over there and I will start."

There was a small squabble as Hannah stood in the wrong place. Then Marie piped up again.

"The Lord said to Moses, go to Pharaoh and say to him let my people go so that they may worship me. If you refuse to let them go I will plague your whole country with frogs. The Nile will teem with frogs."

I sat up straight and took notice. Marie was quoting the bible verbatim. She continued.

"Then the Lord said to Moses tell Aaron, stretch out your hand with your staff and make frogs come up on the land of Egypt." There was a pause. "Now Hannah point your stick and say frogs," hissed Marie in a stage whisper.

"Frogs," said Hannah obediently.

"Pharaoh you jump around trying to kill all the frogs," said Marie to Joe.

I snuck over to the window and peered out quietly. Joe draped in a stripy beach towel, looked at her blankly as he sucked two fingers. At two he did not have much sense of the dramatic. It did not matter. Pharaoh was like a bridegroom.

It was enough he wore the headdress. Marie could plague Egypt without him as easily as she got married without a groom. The longer I listened, the more astonished I became. The bible flowed out of my daughter's mouth as she acted out the story. Perhaps her memorization had something to do with our inefficiency. We meant to go through the bible methodically. But usually, one tape played over and over, for a week or more, before we moved on. It was hard to believe the children dishing out plagues of flies, gnats, and frogs were the same kids who could not remember 'The Lord is my shepherd.' It just proved that the most effective way for kids to learn is often the easy informal way.

What did it matter if we did no bible memorization? What did it matter if family devotions died?

Why move bricks with a wheelbarrow when a conveyer belt is available?

I listened in wonder as Marie continued quoting the Bible fluently.

"Then the Lord said to Moses, tell Aaron, stretch out your staff and strike the dust of the ground and throughout the land of Egypt the dust will become......"

"POOHS!" shouted Hannah with excitement, as she banged her stick up and down. Apparently, Hannah went to sleep before the curse of gnats. I laughed. Hannah's plague was terrible indeed. Perhaps Pharaoh might have let the Israelites go sooner if sewerage had doused Egypt instead of gnats!

Eating a Light Bulb does not make you Bright

The Miracle Swirl

"Put your finger under the word as you read Marie, like I keep telling you to," I said in exasperation. "What's the dog's name?"

Marie looked at me blankly.

"How is it you don't remember the dog's name? We have been going over this for months," I snapped. "Sound it out. Listen T-i-p T-i-p……… TTTTTT iiiiiiiii pppppp."

"Tip?" said Marie uncertainly.

"Tip! That's right! Carry on."

"Come Tip come. Run Tip run. Tip can lie down," read Marie in a monotone.

"No! Don't guess. There is only one word. Lie down is two words, sound it out. J-u-m-p."

It had been like this for years! We did not seem to be making any progress. Every September the nightly guilt escalated to near panic. Her birthday was looming up again. At almost ten, her reading sat at a six-year-old's level.

"Marie will be ten at the end of the month and she still

can't read even basic things," I wailed to Ian.

"What do the Moore's say about late readers?" asked Ian cunningly.

"That some children don't read before eleven or twelve," I said, as Ian knew I would. He only asked because he knew I needed to say the words 'don't read before eleven or twelve.'

"There you go then. Marie is not abnormal."

"But she is not a boy," I wailed. "It is mainly boys that are slow to get the hang of reading."

"There must be girls who struggle or boys couldn't outnumber them," said Ian reasonably. "Do they say only boys struggle?"

"No."

"There you go. You need to read Better Late than Early again."

It was good advice. I got out the well-thumbed book and flicked to the part on late readers. It was more than just an opinion. What they had to say was backed by thirty years of research. I held onto their words the way a drowning man clutches a life raft.

Marie wafted into the room. I hope she had not overheard us talking about her I thought anxiously.

"Hannah learns in steps and stairs but I learn in swirls," she informed me in a cheery little voice.

She obviously had overheard. Fortunately, she did not look damaged.

"I'm a swirly learner."

"What is a swirly learner?" I asked mystified.

"I can't do things. Then I have a swirl, and suddenly I can."

I remembered her learning to ride a bike. She was completely hopeless for a long time. Then bang, she could

Eating a Light Bulb does not make you Bright

ride.

A swirly learner. How true and how depressingly few swirls we had seen! They were rare oases in big dry deserts.

She did not get the swirl thing from me. I was a definite step and stair learner. Trying to build knowledge by gradual layers was hopeless with a swirly-whirly. I had wrestled with her strange brain long enough to feel defeated. It would not be bullied, corralled or tamed. It had its own schedule. If it was not interested, it merely labeled the information as irrelevant and dumped it. Unfortunately, reading was not the only thing Marie was behind in; maths, spelling, science, and dish-washing were all lacking. The child was almost entirely right brained. She was on the high end of the bell curve in art, intuition, social intelligence, and spirituality. In drawing, storytelling or people interaction, Marie excelled. But anything else, forget it! Trying to teach her was a nightmare.

"I am a terrible teacher," I wailed to Ian many evenings. "I just can't get it together with Marie."

"Don't worry Wend. I was exactly the same. I really struggled academically when I was young. Just keep our kids out of school. I don't want them convinced they are dumb the way I was."

"You're right," I said thinking back to our early marriage. "I remember how deep that lie was. You really believed you were dumb. And yet you went on to gain two Masters Degrees in Science and numerous other qualifications."

"The acorn doesn't fall far from the oak," said Ian. "Marie will read when she is ready."

"I suppose so," I said comforted. "You didn't show promise until you were thirty-two. It's silly to expect our children to be early learners."

"Early is not necessarily better," said Ian wisely. "There is nothing wrong with being a late bloomer."

"That's true," I agreed. "I was talking to Sue the other day. She told me her son Jamie didn't read until he was twelve. Then suddenly he went from reading nothing to reading chapter books."

"Maybe Marie will be like that," said Ian encouragingly.

"Maybe," I said doubtfully. "Do you think late blooming could be linked to longevity genes?" I asked, thinking of an article on cattle I had read earlier in the day.

"Whatever makes you think that?" asked Ian.

"I was reading about Texas Longhorns. They look like the cows you see in documentaries on India. They are slower to mature but they live longer than other breeds. Perhaps there is a link between speed of development and life-span?"

"If that is the case," laughed Ian, "our kids will be super late bloomers."

"That's what I was thinking. I don't know another family whose Grandma lived to one-hundred-and-five."

"Remember the time she got stuck up the peach tree when she was ninety-five?" said Ian.

"Yeah," I laughed, "and your great aunty who died at one-hundred-and-six."

"All the others of that generation died in their late nineties," said Ian.

"That's good, all my family go in their eighties," I said happily. "That means I will go before you."

"Not the way I drive," said Ian mischievously.

Despite Ian's encouragement, my panic continued to arise as Marie's birthday loomed closer. The double digits of this year made it seem so much worse. We were at the thankless task of reading again.

Eating a Light Bulb does not make you Bright

Bang! "I can read all of it!"

Wendy Hamilton

"Come Tip come. Tip lie down," Marie read in a bored monotone.

"Not lie down Marie, sound it out. J-u-m-p."

I looked at Hannah's adventure storybook lying on the lounge floor. She was nearly two years younger than Marie, yet Hannah could read much harder books. How many jumps did the blasted Tip have to make, and how many skies had to fall on stupid Chicken Little's head, before the miracle swirl happened?

I felt like a mother bird working very hard to bring educational worms into the nest, only to have her baby birds shut their beaks tightly. Hannah's handwriting was atrocious while six-year-old Joe regularly hid his schoolbooks. Mercifully, I did not yet know that three-year-old Mark would be the worst of all. I thought about education over the centuries. Schools as we know them are a recent idea. How did Sarah, many thousands of years ago educate Isaac? By the time she had pitched her tent, made the family clothes, slaughtered the calf, skinned and gutted it, gathered the firewood, lit the fire, cooked it and drawn water from the well, there would not have been much time for schooling. And yet there is plenty of evidence ancient people were literate.

There had to be another way, the mother bird method required too much time and was too exhausting. As my kids seemed to have the intelligence of vegetables, I would teach them as if they were cabbages. Plant them in good soil and expect them to draw out the nutrients they needed. From now on, I would put all my energies into providing a rich learning environment and let the kids explore the avenues that interested them. Instead of trying to impose set learning on them, I would sit in the backseat to support learning and

Eating a Light Bulb does not make you Bright

enrich their world. Forget silly Chicken Little and stinking Tip. I would make an exciting library in the attic, have story tapes to read along with books. I would read them the classics I used to love; Black Beauty, Little Women, and others. We would have treasure hunts where you had to read to move on to the next clue. Math could be board games and shopping. We could go to museums, and parks, and camp in the bush. I would give up trying to teach like a school and we could just have fun exploring and living. There would of course, still be the chores of cooking, cleaning, painting, and gardening. I had no intention of being Little Red Hen with spoiled lazy chickens. After all, I had my own projects and fun things I to do. Handwriting and worksheets could be done on wet days for the sake of my sanity and the health of the furniture. In our damp climate that should be plenty.

My thoughts were interrupted by a loud laughing coming from the lounge. I peeped in the door. There was Marie curled up in the window seat with her nose deep in a novel!

"Mum I can read this!" she said excitedly. "I just sat down and BANG, I could read all of it!"

I looked at her shocked. It was hard to believe that the same girl who could not read jump a few hours ago, could be reading a chapter book.

"Read this paragraph," I said picking out a portion at random. "But the Queen who was no longer attending to him clapped her hands. Instantly the same dwarf whom Edmund had seen with her before appeared," read Marie fluently.

'Better Late than Early' had said that this sort of thing could happen with late readers, and now I was seeing it with my own eyes. It was a miracle. I could stop panicking and enjoy Marie's birthday. The impossible had happened. Marie had had a swirl. Suddenly she could read!

Wendy Hamilton

What About Socialization?

"You've got your shoes on the wrong feet again, Joe. Can't you feel they are wrong?"

I bent down and swapped the offending footwear around.

"Now hold on to the side of the stroller."

"Hannah, put the cat down! Open the gate for me, please."

"Marie, what have you done with your cardigan?"

"I forgot it."

"Go back and get it." I unlocked the front door again. "Hurry up don't take too long."

I looked at my watch. It was ten o'clock. I was glad I did not have to get the kids to school. It was hard enough to get everyone out the door by ten or eleven without the pressure of having to be somewhere on time.

It took several attempts to get a cardigan that fitted. Eventually, however, we passed through our front gate. As

Eating a Light Bulb does not make you Bright

we walked down the road, I instructed my children.

"Now, when we see the big man in the pet shop, Marie, don't say in a loud voice that man is fat."

"But he is fat," said Marie.

"O.K. I agree he is fat, but there are some things you just don't say even if it is the truth. It is too hurtful."

"It is clever of him to be that fat. I thought he would be pleased about it." Marie looked at me with wide eyes of astonishment.

"I know you thought it was a compliment, but he won't be as happy about it as you think. Trust me on this one!"

I turned around and called out to Hannah. "Hurry up don't dawdle." I waited until she caught up. "And Hannah if a lady in a shop smiles at you, I want you to look her in the eye and say hello. Don't put your finger in your mouth and hide behind me. You may be shy but that does not excuse you from being polite. You don't have to have a whole conversation like your sister would, just say hello. If you burst into tears, you will make the lady feel bad."

I noticed Joe had let go of the stroller and was drifting towards the road.

"Joe, don't walk so close to the curb! A car could come around the corner fast and collect you. Come back here and hold on to the side of the pushchair."

I made sure he was safe before turning back to Marie.

"Marie, when I'm talking to another adult, don't interrupt. If it is really important, put your hand quietly on my arm. I will talk to you when there is a break in the conversation. And don't pat my arm for attention that drives me nuts."

I marshaled my kids along the street instructing them in the delicate art of socialization as we walked. I stopped at a haberdashery and rummaged about in the bargain bin for cotton lace. The woman behind the counter smiled at us.

"Out shopping today," she said conversationally. "My, you girls look pretty in your blue pinafores!"

I poked Hannah as she started turning towards me.

"Say thank you," I hissed. "Say it." I poked her again.

"Thankyoo," mumbled Hannah slurring the words together in her haste to get the dreaded deed over and done with before hiding behind me. I smiled at the lady. At least Hannah had managed the thank you. I was content with one victory. Now was not the time to insist on more. Meanwhile, Marie was talking.

"And I have another blue dress at home and a red dress with spots on it and...."

A million words were tumbling out of her mouth. If I did not check her she would go on and on. Already the woman looked dazed.

"That's nice Marie but I don't think the lady wants to hear about all the clothes in your closet. Sit down quietly on the floor and look at this book." I pulled a picture book out of the baby bag hanging off the handles of the stroller.

"Is it school holidays today?" the woman asked as she measured out two meters of lace.

"Oh no, they are home-schooled."

"Home-schooled?" There was surprise in her voice. She collected herself. "I have a sister-in-law whose daughter is home-schooling," she said snipping the lace with a small pair of scissors. "The kids seem quite advanced. The boy is doing maths I couldn't manage."

I smiled, nodded, and waited. Here it comes, I thought silently, one... two... three.

"I think home-schooling is very good academically but…….."

Eating a Light Bulb does not make you Bright

Wait for it, I thought.

"What about socialization?" she ended in a heavy disapproving tone.

Ahhhhhhhhhhhhhh. There it is. It always comes up.

I thought about my own school days. Why is herding children into packs of thirty peers (all born in the same year) considered a reflection of normal society? I remember the rigid age boundaries you did not cross at school. If the kid was a year older or younger than yourself, you did not associate with them. Even my sister and I did not speak to each other on the school ground. It was hard to integrate the school and home world when a friend came for a visit. Then there was the pecking order. The small world we lived in operated in a separate sphere to the one the teachers inhabited. The powerful kids ruled the playground with the intimidation of Hitler and the immunity of a diplomat. Think back to your own childhood. We all remember a two-faced kid who pulled the wool over the teacher's eyes.

And what about peer dependency and copycat suicides?

Has anyone actually thought through this deeply emotive socialization question?

I reject the implication that a classroom of seven-year-olds can do a better job of socializing my child than I can. And I resent the Government for using education to force political propaganda on children.

I could not say all this to the woman behind the counter, however.

"I think socialization can best be taught at home," I replied defensively.

She did not look convinced, and I left the shop feeling upset. This would not do. Most people have not given any thought to the question. They just reacted to anything that is different. I had to take another approach.

I pondered on it as we walked along the road; past the Baptist church, past the corner dairy, and past the coffee shop with small tables spilling out into the street. Next to the coffee shop was a second-hand shop. It was my favorite shop. I always called in if I was passing. It was small, made smaller by all the stuff squashed into it. The store was aptly named Junk and Disorderly. An unusual chair caught my eye and I strode in briskly. Or rather, I tried to stride in briskly; a stroller and three kids slow things up a bit.

"How much is the chair?"

"Fifteen dollars."

"Good I'll have it."

"Is your car close?" asked the owner of the shop.

"No, I'm walking." I lifted the chair and felt its weight.

"It's alright, it is quite light and I live nearby. Marie can push the baby and I will carry it."

"Good on you, Mum's helper today," said the woman smiling at Marie kindly.

"Is it school holidays?"

"No, they are home-schooled."

"Really! Why don't you send them to school?

The primary school over the road is supposed to be a good one?" Her tone was disapproving.

I took a deep breath. "Because of all the negative socialization," I said with authority in my voice.

I sensed an immediate shift, and suddenly she was on my side.

"So wise. My sister's son goes to the school down the road. He comes home every day crying. The boy in the desk behind him breaks all his pencils and bullies him at lunchtime. And my neighbor's little girl's lunch is stolen every day.

Eating a Light Bulb does not make you Bright

"Say thank you," I hissed.

Her mother has seen the Principle about it but they can't do anything to stop it. Did you hear there was another high school shooting in America?"

She went on and on. It was hard to get around to the business of paying for the chair she was on such a roll.

As I carried my purchase home, I realized I had stumbled on the answer to the dreaded 'socialization' question. Hit it head on and make it your primary reason for home-schooling.

As I turned into my gate, a car backed out of the neighboring driveway.

"Joe, stop it," I said, intervening in a silent social-interaction. "We don't poke tongues out at other people. It is very rude!"

"But he started it!" whined Joe pointing at a small boy in the vehicle.

"I don't care who started it. Look the other way," I said putting my new chair on the veranda.

As I turned the key in the front door and herded everyone inside, it occurred to me it is folly to think a pack of barbaric kids can teach socialization better than a mother."

Eating a Light Bulb does not make you Bright

A Seminar a Birthday and a Boy

Who was it that said, 'I remember how I got kids I just don't remember why'? I was having the same trouble.

"Haven't you been clever, two of each," was a joke I had heard more than once. I far preferred it to the crude one about us not having television. While it was true, we did not own a T.V. that had nothing to do with the birth of Joe and Mark. We had planned to have four children from early marriage. Today, however, I had forgotten why we had Joe.

Our eldest son was getting too big for his boots. That boy needs his chain yanked! I thought angrily. He is getting so naughty. It's probably connected with his birthday coming up.

I had spotted this strange phenomenon before. It was not merely the excitement of presents and a party. It was deeper than that. I had encountered it first with Marie. Directly after her birthday, she often became arrogant and pushed the boundaries. She wanted to see if the rules still applied now that she was officially older. At four, turning five, I thought Joe was rather young to be trying it out. But then I remembered the terrible trouble I had with him over dusting the hall table when he was two. That small inoffensive table was my children's Waterloo. The battleground where two wills wrestled for dominance. Each child, in turn, had fought with me and eventually yielded obedience. Joe also had surrendered, but it had been a long and hard fight. There were still skirmishes, but I was the boss.

The doorbell tinkled. I could see my mother's outline through the rippled glass of the front door.

"Hello Dear," she said as I swung it open. "I'm just popping in with Joe's birthday present." She handed me a supermarket bag wrapped around something lumpy that felt like a plastic car. (Mum did not believe in fancy wrapping paper for a five-year-old.)

"I had a parcel from Brenda this morning. She sent me this," said Mum, holding up a thin oblong. "Look at this darling little chocolate bar with the wee-Scottish-laddie in his little kilt."

We crowded around her and looked at the label. A small boy, standing on the word Edinburgh, stared back at us. "Wasn't it nice of my sister! She and Barry loved Edinburgh, said it was the best part of the trip. I thought you could share it with everyone at Joe's party, but be careful with the wrapper. I would like it back so I can scrapbook it."

When Mum left, I put the present on the top shelf of my closet as Joe's birthday was still a couple of days away.

"Now kids, you heard Grandma say that we could eat this chocolate at Joe's birthday," I reminded them. "Wasn't that nice of her?" Three heads nodded, while Marie started

Eating a Light Bulb does not make you Bright

to explain in depth why it was nice.

I held up my finger and gave Marie a hard look. "It's very special because it has come all the way from Scotland," I said talking over the top of my verbose daughter. "But she wants the wrapper back. I am going to put it in the fridge so the ants won't get it. I don't want anyone touching it. Are you all listening? I don't want anyone touching it," I repeated.

There was a general clammier as everyone vowed not to touch Grandma's chocolate.

I put the chocolate-bar carefully in the side of the fridge door, well away from the sauce bottle that always seemed to tip over and leak.

I turned my attention from Joe's birthday to the weekend. It was time once again for the annual home-schooling seminar. The registration form asked for examples of schoolwork for display. Our family's schoolwork was not worth showing, but our crafts were great. I thought of the cute cart my dad and the kids had made. It would display them beautifully. We called it the popcorn cart because the kids sold popcorn from it. My father had pre-cut the plywood carcass so they could help knock it together. It had a canopy and an attractive handle Dad made on his lathe. The cart rolled smoothly on two bicycle wheels. When it was stationary, a small wooden wheel at the front kept it stable. Under strict supervision, the kids painted it dark green. I, however, with complete freedom, embellished it with bows and swirly whirls.

"Marie and Hannah," I called. There was a stampede of feet as they ran down the hallway. "Bring me all the crafts you've done. I want the small quilt you made with Auntie Antoinette," I said looking at Marie. "And the rag dolls we made last month. Hannah, find the bread-dough bears you made. Have a good look at the bottom of the toy-box. But before you do that, I want you both to pull the popcorn cart out of the garage. I'm going to take it tomorrow."

They rushed off. I heard them rattling about in the garage. Eventually, the rattling changed into thumping as the girls hauled the cart up the steps and onto the back veranda. By the time I had cleaned it up, they had found a stack of things to go on it. I spread Marie's quilt over the top shelf and hung rag dolls off the canopy poles. The more crafts I put on it, the more impressive it looked.

"Do you think anyone will notice we have no written work?" I asked Ian later that night when the kids were in bed. "I'm too embarrassed to display their school books. Marie's spelling looks like Swahili and Hannah's handwriting is terrible."

"You can hardly expect them to be brilliant at spelling when we are both terrible at it," said Ian.

"Yes, we are," I agreed. "And so is my father and sister, and her son and all Dad's brothers. When she was little, I thought Marie might take after Mum and be good at spelling, because her vocabulary was so advanced."

"The only thing she's inherited is the mouth," said Ian darkly.

"Yes, and that has made the problem worse. She uses words like pneumonia and paraphernalia in her stories."

"That does make it tricky," agreed Ian.

"You still haven't answered me. Do you think anyone will notice no schoolbooks?"

"I'm sure they won't," said Ian. "And even if they do, it doesn't matter."

The next day at the seminar, the cart looked good. So good, in fact, a newspaper reporter took a photo of it.

Eating a Light Bulb does not make you Bright

Despite this thrill, I was depressed. There was so much talent surrounding me. It would take weeks to get over the unit study on Israel that the Rushbrook family had done. Their kids were the same age as mine. I looked at the beautiful handwriting and spelling. It was better than I could do. And unlike Violet Blast's bread study, the children had really done it. I noticed vaguely they had no crafts on display. Who cared with writing like that! Another family had done an awesome science experiment. You would think with Ian's background in science, we could have done something along that line. But like Grandma's spelling, scientific acumen was sadly lacking; as was mathematics, and sports. The more I walked around the more depressed I got. I did not realize that I was comparing my children's weakest areas with the other children's strongest points. At the end of two days, my head was spinning. In this state of confusion, I bought a stack of books, hoping for a miraculous way to hammer spelling and maths into my kid's heads.

At the end of the seminar, I heaved the cart into the back of the van and drove home to put together a birthday party.

Joe's party was only a small family one, but I wanted it to be nice. The pinnacle of the party was fancy ice cream sundaes. I set six tall parfait glasses along the bench and spooned ice-cream, and jelly, trifle, and jellybeans into them. I rattled about in the pantry until I found the chopped nuts and glazed cherries. As I reached into the fridge for the cream, I noticed with a sinking heart that Grandma's wee Scottish laddie was missing.

"Marie Hannah Joe and Mark," I yelled, "which one of you has taken Grandma's special chocolate?"

Wendy Hamilton

The popcorn cart.

Eating a Light Bulb does not make you Bright

There was a stampede down the hallway as everyone other than Joe came rushing to me shouting,

"NOT ME NOT ME."

"Where is Joe?"

"In the back room being naughty," three voices yelled gleefully.

I found him covered in chocolate, the ruined wrapper still in his hand.

How could I face my mother?

"You have been a very naughty boy, Joe. For that, you will go to bed early and miss your party."

I was in a black mood as I warmed up his alternate dinner of canned beans. The weekend had been a disaster. My children were below average in everything! And Joe was getting very disobedient. There was, however, one bright spot. I had a lovely newspaper clipping. The story about our family was nice, and the kids looked angelic standing around the cart. I could photocopy it and send one to each set of grandparents. Maybe Mum could scrapbook that instead of the cute Scottish kid. I hunted about for the clipping and found it thrown on the lounge floor. To my horror, Marie, Hannah, and Mark's eyeballs were all blackened out. Moreover, long mustache's and little goatees sprouted from their faces giving them a truly demonic look. Joe alone stood unblemished.

I glared at the shut bedroom door. I was not up to wrestling with that child at that moment. I will deal with him in the morning I thought, as I rammed a paper crown on my head and stomped off to his party. He may have ruined the picture, wrecked the wrapper, and eaten the chocolate, but I still had his ice cream sundae. I smiled savagely, as I ate the cherry off the top.

Wendy Hamilton

The Education Review Office

I ran my fingers along the spines of the books in the bookcase. Which artist should I display this week? Perhaps it was time for a change. I reluctantly bypassed the Impressionist painters. It was easy to thrash the style I liked best. Renoir's paintings stayed before our eyes for a month or more. Unlike Picasso, who only got a brief showing; I did not like the distorted paintings of Cubism. The kids did not like them either. In common with all children, they naturally gravitated to beauty and order. A four-year-old is the first to object to the idea of placing a nose above an eyeball. My hand slowed as I moved over the Dutch painters. Maybe we could look at Van Eyck this week? Suddenly my finger stopped and I pulled out a volume. I could not go past Rembrandt. He was the supreme artist. I loved his black backgrounds and candlelit faces. I found a superb example and slid the open book into my recipe holder. The Apostle Paul smiled

Eating a Light Bulb does not make you Bright

out of the page as I carried him into the kitchen and put him in a prominent position on the bench. This was such an easy way to familiarize my children with great works of art. I got the idea at the home-schooling seminar in an art workshop.

"Famous paintings are often put on postcards," said the speaker. She held up a miniature Mona Lisa. "Display a different one each week to familiarize your children with them."

I thought it was a marvelous idea because it was easy. Moreover, it was a subject I found interesting. I did not know where to get postcards but I had a windfall, however, in the form of someone throwing out a stack of art history books. I scooped them up for a few bucks, removed the rude pictures and displayed them regularly. As I tweaked The Apostle Paul a little to the left, so the light caught him better, Mozart finished doing his thing. The CD had come to an end. Instead of violins, the treble of children's voices filtered down the hallway.

"Go directly to jail, do not pass go and do not pick up two hundred dollars."

There was an annoyed squeal and then a gleeful giggle.

"Well at least I won't be landing on Mayfair, so I won't have to pay you a thousand dollars to stay in your crummy motels!"

There was a rattle of dice.

"Six and five, that's eleven. Haha, you land on my railway station, pay up."

"No, I don't have to pay you because you are in jail."

"Yes, you do!"

"Nah hah, no I don't. Look at the rules."

I pressed replay on the CD player and Mozart obliterated the details of the game. If the arguing was quieter than violins and arpeggios, I did not intervene. It would escalate I knew. The inevitable end to the game was a big fight and tears. Monopoly, always finished that way. In the meantime, however, spontaneous math's, reading and socialization was going on. The attitude 'if it ain't broke yet, don't fix it' worked well for Monopoly.

There was a small clunk as the postman slowed his bike and dropped a letter into the box. Immediately Mayfair and motels were forgotten as the kids rushed outside. They returned en masse and the winner of the race handed me an official-looking letter. I recognized the Education Review Office stamp and took it reluctantly. I had won the E.R.O. ballot at last; a sweepstake nobody wanted to win.

Unlike schools that were reviewed yearly, New Zealand home-schools are picked at random. It was unusual to receive more than one review ever. It simply wasn't cost effective. Moreover, home-schooling families, are low risk. There has never been a case of truancy or drug dealing in any home-school. Neglectful parents do not apply for exemptions or want the hassle of training their children.

I slit the envelope open and quickly scanned the document. A review officer would call on me in three days time at four in the afternoon. A sinking feeling came over me; the depression that close contact with government bureaucracy inevitably brings. I was glad I had my column cash books up to date.

"I am unlikely to have problems," I said to Ian later that night, "but I feel vulnerable knowing the E.R.O. has the power to revoke my exemptions."

"Don't worry about it Wend, remember the woman from the E.R.O. office who spoke at the home-schooling seminar."

"Oh yeah, she said the officers considered going to

home-schools a perk of the job."

"That's right. And how many people do we know who have lost their exemptions?"

"None, now you come to mention it."

"I think we should view this officer as a guest, and on our side. After all……. what's her name?"

I looked at my letter.

"Helen Robinson."

"After all, Helen wants the best for our kids like we do. She is not the enemy."

"You are right."

For the next few days, I went through the house and assembled everything I could think of that related to education. I was glad Helen was coming soon. I did not have time to be nervous. By four o'clock on Wednesday, I was ready. Marie had made Helen a little posy from the garden, and Hannah had written 'Welcome Helen' in wobbly writing on a piece of cardboard. The house was clean and tidy and the boys were outside playing quietly in the backyard. The review office had made it very clear that they were not interested in children under the age of six.

Spread across the kitchen table in neat piles were my resources. The art history books were there of course. As was the Monopoly board, Snakes and Ladders, jigsaws times-table tapes, Letterland textbooks, flashcards, spelling lists, World Vision DVDs, reading books, and handwriting exercise books. I even had some math's workbooks. I did not use workbooks as teaching tools, but they made great rewards for lessons already learned. Hannah, in particular, loved filling out the boxes and putting stickers in the right places. The sheer volume of stuff on display was impressive. It even impressed me. I had no idea I had so much educational stuff in the house. I was particularly fond of the large assortment of crafts that covered half the table. I cleared a space in the center and tenderly laid my column cash books in pride of place. All our activities for the last five years were documented in educational jargon for this very moment. I looked at my watch. Five o'clock, and Helen was still not here. I wonder if she is coming? At least Ian is home from work now I thought. There was a knock on the door.

"Sorry I am late. I got held up," said a plump friendly woman.

"Don't worry about it anyone who deals with people, especially children, is going to have delays," I said. "Welcome to our home. I'm Wendy and this is my husband Ian. We are glad to have you. This is Marie who is ten and Hannah who is eight."

"Hello girls my name is Helen, would you like to show me what you have been doing?"

"This is for you," said Marie handing Helen a posy, "and Hannah's made you a card. Come and see our schoolwork."

Marie led Helen with confidence into the kitchen.

"This is my handwriting book."

"Very nice," said Helen. "Can you find a book and read to me?"

Marie chose a story and started to read correcting herself when she made a mistake.

Outside the window, there was a commotion. I looked out but I could not see what the boys were excited about. They had been very good occupying themselves for over an hour which was good going. I wondered nervously how long it would be before things deteriorated greatly. Hannah took a turn at reading but I listened with only half an ear. Outside the commotion settled down. I refocused my attention on the interview.

"So how do you monitor the girl's progress?" The question was directed at me.

I only have four children and I am with them all the time. It is very easy to know where they are at," I said. "I don't need tests and exams because it is so one-on-one."

She nodded.

"My husband and I have renovated this house by ourselves. We crawled over the roof, painted all the outside, wallpapered all the inside. We have replaced the piles and removed any rot. We know this house intimately because we have worked on it for years. We know our children even better, their strengths, and weaknesses, and where they are at academically?"

She nodded again. "You restored the house yourselves?"

"Yes."

"You've done a good job."

She quizzed me a bit more about my views on education.

"Would you like to hear the girls play a tune?" I asked. I could see them waiting patiently with their recorders and music books.

"That would be very nice."

As 'Silent Night' trilled through the air, the commotion outside swelled and burst through the back door into the kitchen. The concert stopped abruptly.

"Look what Mark found in the back shed," shouted Joe.

A mummified rat dangled from my three-year-old's chubby fist like a grotesque dried fig

"Get it out of here," I shrieked.

"I'll deal with this," said Ian. He ushered Mark out. I heard him through the window insisting that Mark throw his treasure in the compost. By the time the boy's hands were washed and disinfected, Helen had finished.

"A little light on the written work for Social Studies," she said smiling at me, "but on the whole, a well thought out education." She glanced at her watch. "Just look at the time, seven o'clock. I have been here an hour longer than I should have it has been so enjoyable."

As we waved our new friend off, I felt joy and relief. We had passed. The dreaded E.R.O. visit was over and it had gone well. In the midst of this sunshine was a small cloud. After all those years of recording our days in educational jargon, Helen never once looked at my column cashbooks!

Eating a Light Bulb does not make you Bright

Birthdays and a Wish

When I was thirteen my parents bought forty acres on the ridge of Mount Tiger. Technically Mount Tiger is smaller than a mountain, and there is no tiger. It is, however, taller than a hill and rumors have it that the tiger escaped from a circus.

It is a wonderful place.

When Marie turned ten, my parents generously gave us thirty acres of their land; twenty-nine acres of steep bush and one acre of grass with spectacular views.

We ate Marie's birthday cake under a spreading tree on our new land and visualized a small weekend cottage. Two months later, a building site flattened the top of the hill.

The sun was blistering hot as Ian, the girls and I, dug the foundations. Nearby Mark and Joe played with small trucks in a large pile of gravel. "Mum can we have a rest?" whined Marie leaning on her shovel.

"Good idea," I said straightening my aching back. "It is morning tea time. Marie, get the thermos flask out of the van. Hannah, bring up the biscuit tin. There is a blanket on the backseat, spread it out under the trees we will be there in a minute."

I dug my spade into the trench once more. From the corner of my eye, I could see my father checking the taut string lines stretched between the four corner profiles. He was measuring the depth of the foundations. Funny how life cycles around. Across the valley was the quarry my sisters, mother, and I, dug in when Dad was building the home of my childhood.

"How is it that I managed to avoid marrying a builder but I am still slogging at building projects?" I asked my father as we trudged down the hill towards food and shade.

"It's all in the DNA," he replied with a twinkle in his eye. "There is no escaping the family-building-gene."

I sighed, "how true!" My marriage so far was a sea of building projects; without the expertise of a carpenter husband.

We reached the blessed cool of the trees and slumped down on the blanket.

"Admit it you love it," said Ian grabbing a bottle of water.

"It's much better when you're the one getting the building," I admitted. "It is still a beastly job, but the pain seems worth it."

"Do we have to keep helping?" whined Marie. "It's not fair that the boys get to play while Hannah and I have to dig."

"The boys are too young. Two and five-year-olds are not helpful but big girls of nine and ten are. The quicker we get onto this, the quicker we will have a fun place to stay."

"Could I have a horse, now we have some of Grandma

and Granddad's land?" asked Marie hopefully.

"No," said Ian opening the biscuit tin.

"We'll see," I said cautiously as I poured out a cup of tea and handed it to my father. Some requests needed prayer to be successful.

"Horses are dreadful things," said Ian. "I'd rather have a motorbike, they are less expensive."

"They certainly are dreadful things," echoed Granddad sipping his tea. "They wreck fences and eat four times as much as a cow." He bit into a biscuit with the air of a man who has said everything that needs to be said on the subject.

"Mum had horses when she was a girl," said Hannah, not realizing that the topic was finished.

"Yes and see that gate over there," said Granddad goaded into further protest. He pointed across the paddock to a chewed up wooden structure propped between two sagging fences. "Your mother's horses did that." His tone was grim with disapproval.

Joe and Mark sensing food trundled across the uneven ground towards us.

"I caught Mark as he toddled past me and pulled a packet of baby-wipes from my bag.

"You have to clean your hands before you have biscuits," I said to Joe as I wiped Mark's face and hands.

"Grandma's coming," shouted Hannah pointing to a figure climbing the wire fence.

"How are you getting on?" asked Grandma when she got close enough to speak.

"Good," said Granddad. "We should be ready to pour the concrete floor in a couple of days."

"Do you want a cup of tea Mum?" I asked, putting my cup down.

"No thanks Dear, I had one earlier. So girls, what do you think about all this?"

"We are reliving mum's childhood," said Marie.

"Yes you are," agreed Grandma. "Your mother used to ride her horse around these paddocks. And when she got older, she worked with Granddad in his workshop over there," she said, referring to a shed across the valley.

"Were you a good rider Mum?" asked Marie?

"No, and our horses were old, but it was fun."

"It would be quicker to dig a swimming pool than bury a horse," said Granddad sourly, "and a lot more enjoyable."

"Oh Harold, you never had to bury a horse," said Grandma.

"Yes, but I might have had to."

"Tell us some more stories Grandma," said Hannah jiggling up and down.

"Your mother and her sisters used to put flowers in their ponies' hair and…"

"Just think about it," (Granddad was still grave digging.) "Digging for days and days in the hot sun next to a huge stinking carcass."

"They used to play horse shows," continued Grandma, talking over the top of him.

"Big blowflies in summer," Granddad was on a roll.

"And one day….." Grandma was also on a roll.

"Freezing wind in winter."

"I saw an advertisement in the paper for a horse"

"How would you even get a heavy thing like that into the hole?"

"Free to a good home, so I rang the number and…."

"Wrap chains around it and pull it with the car I suppose.".

"Did you get a free horse?" asked Marie looking excited.

Eating a Light Bulb does not make you Bright

"That's enough horse talk," cut in Granddad hastily. "We don't want to hear the rest of that story Grandma."

"At least she doesn't want a dog," I said changing the subject to something we all agreed on. "Horses are much better than dogs"

"That's right," said Ian. "Dogs stink."

"Yes," said Granddad, "they dig up the garden and eat shoes."

"Dirty footprints all over the carpet," said Grandma.

"Dogs are yucky," said Marie. "Remember that big one that licked my face?"

"Quite right," agreed Granddad in a jovial voice, his temper restored. He picked up his tape measure and headed back up the hill. I sighed, put the lid on the biscuit tin and screwed the cap on the thermos flask. The morning tea break was over.

By the time Marie turned eleven, a small building had grown up out of the rocky foundations. It was basic; one large open plan room with three tiny bedrooms opening off the left wall. There was no electricity, and the outside toilet was down a long pathway. I slid a birthday cake onto the table and made tea out of rain collected from the roof.

"Grandma and Granddad are coming," squealed Hannah looking down the long driveway.

"Where's the birthday girl?" said Grandma as they came in the French doors. She carried a plate of chocolate truffles and a flat parcel.

"Here I am," said Marie, rushing up and giving them a hug as Granddad put some bottles of fizz beside the birthday cake.

"Happy Birthday," said Grandma giving Marie the packet.

"Oooo thank you, Grandma," said Marie starting to rip the Christmas wrapping off.

"Careful now," admonished Grandma, "I want to reuse that paper."

Marie obediently altered course and peeled the sellotape off with agonizing slowness.

"A book on horses, just what I wanted, thank you. See what else I got for my birthday," she added as she snatched a Barbie horse and a plastic stable off the couch.

"That's lovely," said Grandma fiddling absentmindedly with the pink stable door. "Your mother used to like these things when she was your age."

"Now I'm eleven, could I have a real horse for Christmas?" asked Marie looking at us hopefully.

"We'll see," I said cautiously. Some requests needed lots of prayers to be successful.

"No," said Ian predictably. "A horse is a dreadful idea. I'd rather have a motorbike."

"Quite right," said Granddad frowning. "They wreck fences and eat as much as four cows." As usual, he said it as if there was nothing more to say on the subject.

"How old was Mum when she got a real horse?" asked Hannah carrying on recklessly.

"Thirteen. She saved all her pocket money, and birthday, and Christmas money to get one."

"Hmm," said Marie thoughtfully. "Do you think next year I could have money instead of a present?"

"You can save a hundred thousand dollars and you are still not getting a horse," said Ian guessing her thoughts.

Eating a Light Bulb does not make you Bright

"Your father is quite right," said Granddad approvingly.

"I think that is a little bit hard," said Grandma. "Our girls loved their horses."

"You will not be the one to bury it if it dies," said Granddad grimly.

"No, it would be me," said Ian even more grimly.

"Yessssss, it would be you," said Granddad perking up at the novel thought.

"At least she doesn't want a dog," I said changing the subject. "Dogs are filthy animals."

"That's right," said Ian taking the bait. "They stink and leave poops all over the yard."

We waited for Granddad to say, "they dig up the garden and eat shoes," but he just stared into the air.

"So hard on carpets," said Grandma at last. "Dog hair gets everywhere."

"Dogs are yucky," said Marie. "Remember the big one that licked my face and made it all wet?"

"Ian would be the one to dig a hole," said Granddad suddenly. It appeared he had not moved on from burying the horse. And fix all the fences." He paused thoughtfully. "I don't think a pony or two is a bad idea after all," he said looking at Marie indulgently.

"We don't have enough grass for two horses," said Ian looking betrayed.

"No problem, I have plenty," said Granddad pointing at the lush paddocks across the fence.

"They are expensive," said Ian desperately.

"Not always," said Granddad. "Tell everybody how you got a free one, Grandma."

Wendy Hamilton

I Still Want a Horse

Once a month we used our weekend cottage as a church hall. We stuffed all the furniture from the main room into the tiny bedrooms and set out thirty plastic chairs. Marie's twelfth birthday fell on a Chapel Sunday.

As usual, after a very relaxed church service, we shared lunch together.

Neighbors clustered about in small groups, talking and laughing.

They filled the main room and overflowed onto the newly built veranda. I popped Marie's birthday cake into an empty spot on the laden trestle table.

Ting ting ting, Ian rapped a glass to get everyone's attention.

"It's Marie's birthday today, let's all sing Happy Birthday."

Mum stood on her left leg, put her right foot on a chair, and started strumming her guitar. It was amazing how many tunes she could bash out with three chords.

Eating a Light Bulb does not make you Bright

I lit the twelve candles as we sang. The last candle flared as the final Happy-Birthday-to-yoooou finished.

"What did you wish for," shouted someone as Marie blew them all out with one breath.

"A pony," she answered beaming. "That is what I most want in the world."

"You shouldn't have said what you wished for," said Joe, "now it won't happen."

"Good," said Granddad out of habit. "Horses are dreadful things." He said it without his usual conviction, however.

"Yeah, they eat four times as much as a cow and wreck the fences," grumbled Bill who lived up the road.

All the farmers in the room growled in agreement. "Look at Harold's fences, horses did that." Joe pointed through the window at our sagging boundary fence.

"Ian's going to fix them when Marie gets a horse," said Granddad airily.

"She is not getting a horse," said Ian emphatically.

"Yeah right! drawled Norton. "You'll be fixing fences forevermore." He loved to tease Ian.

"Like you have to," said Ian.

"I don't have any horses."

"You have so, you've got four of them. You stuff them in your horse float and take them around all the shows."

"They are not horses, they are miniatures," said Norton doing his best to distance himself from the disgrace. "Besides, they are nothing to do with me, they are Mum's and Clara's."

"Can I have a miniature horse?" asked Marie eyeing Ian and me hopefully.

"No," said Ian. "Horses are dreadful things. I'd rather have a motorbike."

"They are not," said Jeanette indignantly. (It was well known she kept thirteen of them as field ornaments.)

"That's right," said Olivia with the light of battle in her eye. "They teach children responsibility."

The room was polarizing as the divide between for and against heated up. I scanned the sea of dog lovers.

Evelyn had chosen the color of her carpet to match her Rottweiler's hair and dirty paws. My usual distraction was not going to work this time.

"Go on, let your daughter have a pony," said Norton. "A bit of fencing would be good for you. Make you into a real Mount Tiger man."

"Horses are expensive," said Ian ignoring the last remark.

"I've got an old quiet one. Your girls could borrow her for the summer," said Jeanette. "Her name is Sugar because she is very sweet."

"Daddy please can we, please please please?" shouted Marie and Hannah jumping up and down in excitement.

"Go on Ian," said Norton gleefully. "Don't be a spoilsport."

"One summer might be enough to get it out of their system," I said persuasively.

"Oh all right," said Ian caving in. "But only for the summer. And…" he eyeballed Marie with a hard look, "don't think this means you're getting one of your own."

"OK Daddy," said Marie, nodding her head vigorously.

"I'll give you my wire-tighteners," said Granddad looking at Ian in a jovial manner. "They used to belong to my father."

"Wouldn't he be thrilled to know another generation will be using them," said Grandma enthusiastically.

Eating a Light Bulb does not make you Bright

"I'll show you how to use them next weekend," said Granddad beaming.

"Wonderful," growled Ian looking glum.

Have a piece of birthday cake Darls," I said cutting him a big slice.

Wendy Hamilton

Praying for a Horse

Weekends at Mount Tiger were an established way of life by the time Marie turned thirteen. Every Friday night we packed the van with supplies and headed off into the mountains. The routine was much the same from week to week.

"Can someone catch the cats and shut them in the bedroom," I yelled as I struggled out to the van with two violins and a stack of maths books. "I can see Molly slinking away, catch her before she hides. Dad will be home soon. I don't want to spend an hour hunting for her. And someone tie up the rubbish bags and put them out by the curb. Otherwise, we will miss the collection on Monday."

There was a rush of wind as four kids pelted after the cats. Nobody wanted to be the 'someone' to deal with the rubbish.

I put my load on the ground and lifted the van's rear door. A bag of library books cascaded out and scattered over the ground. I sucked in my breath sharply, as 'Brain

Eating a Light Bulb does not make you Bright

Development in Children' clobbered my big toe.

"Why do we always have a bursting vehicle no matter which way we travel?" I asked Marie in exasperation, as she ambled out of the house and over to the van.

"Dunno," she said indifferently as she stomped on Character Training for Preteens.

"Be careful," I snapped, scooping 'Child Rearing A to Z' out of her path.

"Can we have some chooks?" she asked dumping a stack of horse-care books behind the back seat.

"Of course not, we don't live at Mount Tiger all the time," I said putting a young lemon tree by the front tire.

"Dad could make a chicken coop that fits on the trailer so we could take them back and forth like the cats."

"Absolutely not!" The idea of adding chickens to our traveling circus filled me with horror. I loved both places but like the cats, I did not like the trip between town and country.

"Can I have my own horse then? Grandma and Granddad could keep an eye on it when we aren't there."

I sighed. This conversation was years old and not going away. Borrowing a horse for the summer had not diminished the desire for one.

"I would love you to have a horse but you know your father is against it. You would have a lot more success getting a motorbike."

"Could you ask him if I can have one?" My daughter looked at me with pleading eyes.

"Marie, there are some things not even I can get your father to do. This needs lots and lots of prayer. You will have to ask God to change his heart. That is the only way you'll get a horse."

"I'll start asking God tonight then," she said with determination. "And I won't stop until Dad says yes."

Ian's work vehicle pulled into the driveway. Are we all ready to go?" he asked getting out.

"Nearly, all we have to do is get the cats and lock up. It's moments like these I wish I was a dog person," I said bitterly as I slammed the van door. "Cats are a pain to shift around."

"I don't, said Ian. "Dogs are filthy animals. They poop on the lawn, they eat rubbish and you have to register them."

"I don't want a dog," said Marie dumping Molly and Morris in the van. "If a cat licks my face, it's nice."

"That's right," said Ian. "Climb in everybody. I want to get out there before dark." There was a scurry and the sound of seatbelt's clicking. I picked up the lemon tree and climbed in the front seat beside my husband. Ian put the gearstick into reverse and backed out the driveway. The cats howled as we entered the busy traffic.

"Stop at the tomato place," I said spying a large sign in the distance. "They have got boxes of bottling tomatoes on sale."

"Alright, but don't be long," said Ian slowing to a stop.

"Hold on to Molly and Morris," I said to the kids as I balanced the tree on the cupholder between the front seats. I opened the door carefully, whisked out and banged it shut. Getting in again was more difficult because the box was a generous size.

"Here take it," I said to Hannah as I squeezed it into the backseat area.

"Why do I have to hold it?"

Eating a Light Bulb does not make you Bright

"Please Lord, let me have a pony."

"Because Marie is holding the handbasin."

"Can we eat some?" piped up Joe from the furthest back regions.

"Yes but don't dribble them everywhere they are very ripe." I grabbed one out of the box and gave it to Ian before lifting the tree back onto my lap, and buckling up my seatbelt again. Once more Ian pulled out into the traffic. The cats increased their howling. He drove a short distance before turning off into a winding narrow road.

"Can you move that tree, it's in my way?" he said changing gears with difficulty.

I pulled the trunk of the lemon closer to the window.

"I hope the possums won't wreck this tree," I said.

"It is always possible," said Ian. "That is the downside of living in the country."

"Dad said he would come over tomorrow and help us put the bay window in the extension," I said happily.

"That's good," said Ian. "I think we can manage the small side window ourselves but that big one is funny angles. Your father is good how he teaches us instead of just taking over."

"Yes," I agreed. "You've learned so much from him. You're getting pretty good at it. Remember the days you used to choke the hammer? You never hold it around the neck now."

A squabble broke out in the back as I shifted my tree uneasily.

"I don't want it over my side. Your legs are shorter, you can have it," Marie snapped at Hannah.

Legs thumped the back of my seat. I leaned through the gap between Ian and me.

"What is going on?"

"The tool kit is in my way," said Marie. "The wrecking

bar is sticking into me."

"We don't have far to go, pick it up and hold on to it until we get there," I said irritably. I did not want to be bothered with grumbling kids. I had my own difficulties. I could feel damp seeping onto my lap from the sacking wrapped around the tree's roots. The cats who had quietened down started yowling again.

"Joe's annoying the cats," piped up Marie in a self-righteous tone of voice. There was a hiss, and Mark started bawling.

"Joe, stop tormenting the cats, and leave your brother alone," I yelled craning my neck around to eyeball my son.

"I'm hungry," whined Hannah.

"Have another tomato," I said to shut her up. "We are nearly there."

The drive between our two properties was only twenty minutes. Nevertheless, it was a great relief when the van bounced down the Mount Tiger driveway.

"Hurry up and get everything unloaded before we lose the light," said Ian as we all tumbled out.

"Do you really need all those books?" I asked Marie as she lugged her horse books up the pathway.

"Yes, I don't want to run out of reading."

"Isn't it strange," I said to Ian as he unlocked the French doors. "All those years I worried over Marie not reading and now I worry that she is reading too much."

"Don't sweat over it," he said dumping a box of groceries on the table, "there are plenty of things for her to do out here."

"But that's just it," I said, leaving the lemon tree on the veranda, "all she does is read. She is not getting enough exercise."

Wendy Hamilton

God had answered Marie's prayers.

Eating a Light Bulb does not make you Bright

"Can I have a horse?" asked Marie cutting in on our conversation. "I would get lots of exercise if I had a horse!"

"No," said Ian firmly. "You can't have one horse they are a herd animal."

"We could get one for Hannah too," I said hopefully.

"No," said Ian firmly. "Let's drop the subject."

I looked at Marie and shrugged. I knew when I was beaten.

"One more load each and we will be done," said Ian as Hannah trailed up the path with the tomatoes. "Everyone hurry up, it will be dark soon. Mark and Joe, stop playing with the cats and come and help," said Ian bustling out again.

I lit the lamp and heated some stew in a pot on the gas stove as the others brought everything in and packed it away. It was cozy sitting around the table eating in the lamplight. Long shadows stretched like dark fingers up the dim walls. The bedroom doors gaped like black holes. It did not feel creepy, however, especially when the table was cleared and a raucous game of Last-Card was in full swing.

"One more game, then time for bed," I said lighting the candles in the bedrooms.

"Aw Mum, can we have two games?" Joe yelled. "I need to beat Hannah."

"One! I expect to see you all in bed by the time I get back from my shower."

I filled the shower-bag up with warm water and wandered outside to the shower house; a rickety structure Ian and I cobbled together out of pallets and black polythene. I could hear the Moreporks hooting and the kiwis whistling down in the valley below. Above me, the Milky Way swooped across the star-studded sky. It was lovely until a possum screeched.

The kids were in bed by the time I got back. I peeped

into the girl's bedroom.

Soft candlelight illuminated the bunks with their little storybook curtains. Instead of Marie's usual prattle, I could hear her praying.

"Dear Lord, please change Dad's mind and let me have a pony. I'm going to keep asking you until you do. Amen."

Eating a Light Bulb does not make you Bright

Weeds

I put fourteen candles on Marie's birthday cake and covered it with a gauzy tea-cloth. We would have it tonight at her party. The kettle whistled cheerily on the nearby woodstove. As usual, a stack of character training books sat on a small table next to a comfortable couch. We had come a long way in four years. The ugly little building had turned into a charming cottage; a real home away from home. A short distance away, down brick steps, stood a second building. It was our latest building project. Nowadays we spent more time at Mount Tiger than in town. I waved to Ian as he drove down the driveway off to work. In the lounge area, Mark made happy bumble-bee noises as he played with blocks. I could see the girls riding their horses around Granddad's front paddock. God had answered Marie's frequent prayers. It had taken another six months for Ian to come around, but eventually, two ponies, Oscar and Chris, had joined our family. They were young, not old. It was unlikely Ian would ever have to bury them. I made a cup of tea and wandered leisurely outside to the garden seat. The dishes could wait for half an hour while I smelled the roses.

I glanced at my watch; five-past-eight. I heard the Primary School Bus droning in the distance as it labored up a nearby hill. I thought of the books on the small table beside the couch and felt good that my children were not amongst the group waiting for it at the corner. This was such a good environment to bring children up in. Clean fresh air, a slow lifestyle, with plenty of opportunities to mold their characters. The bus slid into view as it breasted a far hill and coasted down. Across a shallow valley, I could see my father showing Joe how to skin a possum. It was a blessing having my parents nearby. I took a sip of my tea and watched the girls idly. It was strange they wanted to ride so early when they had all day. Meanwhile, the bus slid lower until it sunk behind a row of trees. I heard the sharp squeak of brakes and the hiss of the door as it opened for the unfortunate children waiting to get on. The door banged and the motor growled as it picked up speed. It rounded the corner and swung into view. In response, the lazy trotting suddenly burst into a flurry of speed which continued until the bus drove out of sight.

In the still morning air, my children's voices carried easily over the grass.

"Did you see their faces?" crowed Marie naughtily. "They were green with envy."

"Yeah," said Hannah. "All those girls were jealous we could ride while they went off to do math's and spelling!"

So much for Godly character development! It looked like we were nurturing the big show-off weed.

I stood up and cupped my hands around my mouth. "Put your horses away and come inside girls." I hollered.

Eating a Light Bulb does not make you Bright

The lazy trotting burst into a flurry of speed.

"Can we stay out here until the High School Bus goes past," yelled Marie back.

"No."

I sat down again and tapped the seat with my fingers absent-mindedly while I thought about the best way to grub out these particular thistles.

By the time they clumped up the path, bridles slung over their shoulders, I had it.

"I want you girls to wash the dishes. Then you can practice your violins, and write a story on the importance of not showing off. And," I paused for dramatic effect, "at four this afternoon, when the High School bus comes past, you can practice spelling and do a page of division problems each. Do it in the front paddock so all the girls on the bus can see you, and feel smug that they are not doing math's and spelling."

"Aw Mum."

"I don't want to hear any more about it," I said pouring out another cup of tea. I slipped outside again and sat back on the garden seat. I heard the clink of dishes getting clean as I watched the bee's buzzing in and out of the hot pink dahlias.

Contentment washed over me. I loved this simple lifestyle. Close by the horses munched grass noisily. I was so glad we finally had ponies. Only one thing marred my happiness; Mark had started praying for a puppy.

Eating a Light Bulb does not make you Bright

The Silver Lining

It was mid-December. The summer holidays had started. Normally it was hot and dry. This year, however, it looked like we were going to get the white, soggy, Christmas none of us were dreaming of. It had rained solidly for a week. Our cottage perched on the ridge of Mount Tiger was enveloped in white mist. It rose from the valley below and shrouded us in thick fog. When the dirty gray clouds first appeared, I prayed they would not bypass my parched garden. My prayer was answered abundantly. By the end of seven days, they were like visitors who had outstayed their welcome.

My overwhelmed drier broke. Dirty clothes stacked up in smelly damp piles. The kids trekked mud inside. And my plants went moldy with blight.

It was depressing and I was not the only one depressed. The chickens were depressed. The kids had finally persuaded me to let them have two big Orpingtons and two little Araucanas. At first, the hens scratched jauntily in the rain looking for floating worms. Their bustling body language suggested joy in a gourmet dinner. What was a little wetting? But after a prolonged soaking, their interest in bloated worms waned. They moped about and picked their way sadly through puddles. Their under-feathers trailed in the mud. Furthermore, something had happened to their heads. The heads of the big Orpingtons had shrunk. Their necks, however, had swollen up; as if all the feathers on top had slipped down and regrouped into Elizabethan collars. Meanwhile, the heads of the little Araucanas blossomed into spiky bushes as their necks thinned into weedy storks.

Like the chickens, the landscape had also undergone change. The chook's house usually stood under a line of big trees. After days of heavy rain, it was still under the trees. At least, the branches of the trees still spread over it. A moat, however, had sprung up between the trunks and the building. The chicken coop sat like a castle marooned on an island, its drawbridge the only link to the mainland.

By the sixth day of rain, the island had disappeared and the castle had become a hut on a pond; the drawbridge had turned into a boat ramp.

Normally at six in the morning, all four chooks were lined up under Marie's bedroom window awaiting their breakfast. On the seventh morning, they were conspicuously absent. The usual demanding squawks were missing. The veranda was empty. Ginger did not hop onto the rocking chair, and nobody peered through the window. None of the chooks wanted to get out of bed and brave the heavy rain anymore; not even for corn.

Down the road, the neighbor's water tank was overwhelmed. It collapsed with a sonic boom and a tsunami that hurled tree roots and debris down the hillside.

On the eighth day of rain, there was still no sign of

Eating a Light Bulb does not make you Bright

letting up. Despite rising cabin fever and a few spots of temper (noticeably mine), we were trying to keep up the Christmas spirit. During a drought of half an hour, the kids managed to fell and dry (I'm not sure how) a small pine tree. It stood in the corner of the main room awaiting lights. Surrounding it were presents shrouded in home-made wrapping paper. I particularly liked the blue paper bag salvaged from the rubbish-bin and gussied up with a large red bow. It demonstrated ingenuity, and the name of the telephone company looked festive if you used imagination.

A glaring white light penetrated the window. Mark was busy trying to draw a mud-man. Joe meanwhile was composing a song called I'm Dreaming of a Brown Christmas. I sighed. The reasonable expectation of a hot green Christmas seemed slim this year. Maybe it might turn out to be one of those summers that happened occasionally where we skipped the hot dry bit and were doused with a monsoon instead. The farmers LOVED those rare summers, as lots of rain meant lots of money. Mothers, however, hated the wet conditions. For them, it meant summer holidays cooped up with hyperactive kids. On the bright side, it was warm and I did not have to water my fruit trees. Although if the rain kept coming my citrus trees could drown. Certainly, the peaches would swell and burst if they did not develop brown rot first.

"That's stupid," said Joe stabbing his finger on Mark's picture, "you can't make a snowman out of the mud."

"Well your song's dumb," retaliated Mark.

A scuffle broke out. From scuffling it was a small step to fighting and yelling.

"Why don't you kids, pop some corn and string it into long strands?" I intervened. "Popcorn looks pretty draped around a Christmas tree."

I threaded four needles with strong thread, while the girls poured yellow kernels into a hot pan over the wood range.

"And when you girls are finished, you could make wooden peg angels," I added.

"Like the ones, we made last year?" asked Marie.

"That's right, and you boys can cut paper snowflakes. I'll show you how to fold the paper."

I had acted in the nick of time.

The foolish talk subsided. Instead, the room was filled with happy humming noises as we made snowflakes and angels. I thought about our Christmas decorations as we cut paper and threaded popcorn. Snowflakes and snowmen were a silly idea. Christmas for us meant barbeques, boating and lying on a hot beach. Santa bought bikes, and paddling pools, not snowboards, and ice skates. Yet shops sprayed fake-snow around the edges of their windows. Apart from a few cards depicting Santa in swimming trunks, we all decorated with a frosty theme. Department store Santas had it rough at Christmas parades. The back of a truck at mid-day in summer is a bad place for an elderly fat man; especially one wearing a full Santa suit. Perhaps the silly idea of snow in summer had something to do with our youthful country. Scratch the surface of New Zealand and you will find Britain.

By the twelfth consecutive day of rain, things were getting desperate, and I was running out of things to occupy the kids. The tree looked lovely covered in angels, popcorn, and snowflakes. In addition, there were red bows and varnished bread-dough stars. The Christmas cake was baked and five cent pieces were hidden in the plum pudding. The presents were shrouded in mystery, and Joe had composed his own version of The Twelve Days of Christmas.

Eating a Light Bulb does not make you Bright

It started with

"On the first day of rain, my mother said to me, go out and find a Christmas tree."

And ended with

"On the twelfth day of rain, my mother yelled at us, get out of here before I make a fuss."

I laughed at his cheeky stanzas but they gave me an idea.

"Kids, get on your raincoats. We are going for a walk."

Grumbling broke out as everyone pulled on damp boots and coats. They were as reluctant to get wet as the chooks. Once we got down the road a little, however, things perked up.

The road wound up and down through lush bush and pasture, sometimes riding the ridge of Mount Tiger, sometimes clinging to sides of steep hills; a high bank on one side a sickening drop on the other. Where the road sliced through a bulldozer-cutting, ferns clung to the sides of the banks; their vivid green contrasting with the orange clay. As the clouds rose gently from the surrounding valleys, the kids (armed with long sticks) scurried about like dogs out for a walk.

Joe bashed his stick on a branch above Hannah's head. "Got ya!" he shouted as an avalanche of water doused her.

"Got you back," shouted Hannah bashing the tall tree fern above his head.

I kept out of the way as sticks and water flew about. When they tired of that game, they poked in the mud and picked some mushrooms they found growing by a fencepost. We continued meandering along the road like dogs out for a walk until we got to the spotty-horses. It was there that the boys discovered a treasure. While the girls were patting a friendly mare who had wandered up to the fence, the boys found a huge puddle in a wide ditch.

"Hey Mum this is quite deep," called Joe in excitement as he measured the depth with his stick. "Can I get in it? My raincoat is leaking and I am already very wet."

"Oh all right," I replied. "You can't get much wetter than you already are."

There was a chorus of delight as they all decided to try out this tempting waterhole.

"If you sit down, you can get wet up to your neck", said Mark beaming.

I heard a car in the distance coming closer. It rounded the corner and slowed, swinging onto the wrong side of the deserted road. It was Norton. I saw him laughing at the four heads poking out of the brown water. He tooted as he passed before swinging back onto the left-hand side.

We tramped home several hours later, our faces aglow. My children looked like sodden chickens.

The boy's short hair stood on end in prickly wet spikes, while the girl's heads had shrunk. Unlike the chooks, however, a complete soaking had invigorated them and restored morale. I pitied the women who sent their kids to school. The last twelve days were more difficult for them than me. My mother hated school holidays. It was hard for her to have us underfoot when she was used to five peaceful hours every day. Vacations for me merely meant 'business as usual'. I loved the holidays. I did not have to find educational justification for the day's activities or feel bad if we did nothing.

"Two days until Christmas I can't wait," shouted Marie whacking two stones with her stick.

She was not the only one counting down the days. Mothers everywhere were also ticking days off the calendar.

Eating a Light Bulb does not make you Bright

They poked in the mud.

They were not waiting for Christmas, however.

"Five weeks until school starts again."

The first day of school felt more like Christmas to my mother than the twenty-fifth of December.

As we turned in our gate and trudged up the long driveway, the rain stopped. The sun broke through the parting clouds and a rainbow spanned the valley; the bottom of which stopped at our cottage. The tan colored walls of the house glistened like a pot of gold. I smiled. My house had lots of noise and activities going on in it, and home-schooling required extra commitment. There was a silver lining to the frequent dark clouds, however. School holidays held no terrors. You never hear a home-schooling Mum grumble about school holidays. They are not an issue.

Eating a Light Bulb does not make you Bright

Noise Monitoring

The bedroom walls in our country cottage stood naked. They looked gloomy and cold. The white plaster slicked between wallboards and over nails, looked like long bones and spots of skin cancer. It had taken two days to get the walls stripped.

The kids were a big help. Armed with bowls of water and paint scrapers, they had scratched and pulled at the paper until nothing remained.

At night I was filled with guilt when I thought of my column-cash-books. The only box with anything written in it was the History column. And that was only because we listened to an audiobook as we worked. Better Late than Early said that kids who do the best academically are the ones that are involved in practical activities. I sincerely hoped the Moore's were right. My kids thought Pythagoras was a snake. But all of them (including six-year-old Mark) knew that the Underground Railroad was not a subway train.

The next morning, I wiped the kitchen sink quickly

and left the kitchen without sweeping the floor. Ten rolls of wallpaper beckoned me irresistibly. There would be no dictation today. Or any other schoolwork for that matter.

"You kids worked hard yesterday and did a good job, so you may occupy yourselves today. Finish listening to The Underground Railroad and find out if the slaves made it to Canada."

There was a glad flurry as everyone scattered to find pleasant occupations.

"Mum, where is the drawing paper and the colored pencils?" asked Marie." I want to draw a picture of Harriet Tubman guiding the runaway slaves through the forest."

"In the hutch-dresser," I said mechanically. "Mark, before you tip all the blocks over the floor, come and stir this paste for me." I handed him a wooden spoon and pointed to a bowl of water.

"That's right, just stir round and round evenly while I pour the powder in."

I trickled grains of paste into the water and Mark whirled the spoon as I called out instructions to the others.

"Joe, get the folding table from the bottom building and set it up in the bedroom for me."

"Hannah, find the tape measure and wide brush for the wallpaper paste. I think you will find them in Dad's tool kit."

"Marie! I said the hutch-dresser, not the junk-drawer!"

Meanwhile, the spoon whirled less and less energetically.

"No Mark, don't stop, concentrate! It will go all lumpy if you don't keep stirring," I said in exasperation.

Eventually, the paste was made, the table set up, the pencils found, and I had a wide brush.

Marie and Hannah drew while Mark played with blocks and Joe fiddled with wires. I pressed the button on the CD

Eating a Light Bulb does not make you Bright

player and a cultured voice filled the small building. With one ear I listened to the story. With the other, I monitored the kids. I could hear the plastic tinkle of blocks, and the sounds of happy humming, and murmuring. They were constructive engaged sounds.

In the bedroom I measured cut and pasted, making a few happy humming noises myself. At ten o'clock I glanced at my watch.

"Marie put the kettle on please. I will finish this sheet of wallpaper, and then I will come and organize morning tea."

There was a sound of running water. Then a bang and a thump as the lid went on the kettle and the kettle went on the stove. I heard a scrape as Marie dragged the cake tin off the shelf. I put my cloth down, switched off the BBC voice, and headed for the kitchen.

I glanced at the table as I passed. By Marie's chair was a picture of Harriet Tubman skulking through swirls of green pencil. Hannah, scissors in hand, was busily cutting out paper shapes. Ghoulish body parts lay scattered around her.

"Mum. Look at my St John's Ambulance project," she said proudly holding up a paper skeleton.

"That is wonderful Hannah," I said admiring the grisly eyeball, heart, and eardrum pasted in the correct places. "Heart has an E between the H and A," I added, pointing at the mistake. "Good on you for nearly finishing that assignment. Make sure you polish your shoes before Wednesday's cadet meeting."

I sniffed as I cut the cake. A strong singed smell hung about the room.

"Have you turned off the soldering iron and made sure it is not touching anything?" I cautioned Joe as I handed him a piece.

"Of course Mum!" he said, offended that I would ask such a no-brainer. "Look at the light bulb Sean gave me. I've made it go!"

We admired Joe's invention as we munched cake. Mounted on a wooden block was a small Christmas tree light. Wires ran from it to a switch and a battery.

"See, you can turn it on and off," he said demonstrating.

"Well done," I said. "That is amazing! I don't know how you know about that kind of stuff."

I drained my cup and put it on the bench.

"Girls rinse out the cups and clean up any crumbs before you go back to your projects. I am going to start on another wall."

I pressed the play button to resume our story. Once more the constructive bumblebee noises filled the cottage. I pasted happily and the room started to transform. It was going to look great when it was finished. I could not wait to paste the heart border around the middle of the wall. A cute border put the final zing into country décor.

Halfway around the third wall, however, there was an ominous change in the background noise; like a car changing gear as it starts up a steep hill. The noise rose as the behavior dropped. Now the constructive buzz was punctuated with spats of raucous laughter. I felt uneasy; it was the start of the slippery slope. When I was a child, my mother often said

"Stop that silly laughter, it will end in tears."

Back then, I had no idea what she was talking about. Thirty years later, I knew exactly what she meant.

"I don't like the noises I'm hearing. Do I need to come in a investigate?" I shouted threateningly.

"Noooooooo!"

There was a chorus of denial and the silly sounds muted.

Eating a Light Bulb does not make you Bright

"How do you spell kidney?" called Hannah.

"K-I-D-N-E-Y," I spelled slowly.

I carried on papering. Snip, snip……. Paste, paste…….. bang, slide, and smooth. My ears like sensitive radars zeroed into the noises coming from the other room.

"Hannah, stop it, I don't look like that!" whined Marie.

"Haha, yes you do!" yelled Joe.

"You're a pooh Joe, this is how you look!" shouted Marie back.

"Don't do that!" howled Hannah. "You'll wreck my eyeball and I'll have to do it again!"

"Well you shouldn't have called your skeleton, Marie!" shouted her offended sister.

I threw down my sticky brush.

"That's it, you kids!" I said emerging from the bedroom. "I want you to pack away everything and run up and down the driveway ten times."

"She started it," said Marie pointing at Hannah.

"I don't want to hear," I said cutting her short. "You've obviously got too much energy and need exercise." I looked at Mark who was still playing.

"You too Mark, tidy all those blocks away."

I stalked back into the bedroom and picked up my brush again. A thought hit me. I turned back and poked my head through the doorway. "And when you have finished it will be lunchtime, so you can set the table after your run. Move it!" I rolled out a length of wallpaper and started slapping paste on it. I heard muttering and grumbling as the kids reluctantly cleared up. Then there was blissful silence as they scampered up and down the hundred-meter driveway. I figured if I worked quickly I could get one more drop of wallpaper on before lunch time. The phone rang.

"Hello Dear," said my mother, "I wondered if you would like to pop over for a cup of tea?"

The idea of sitting in Mum's childless house seemed very attractive.

"I would love to but I can't stay long because I am wallpapering today. I'll come over after I have fed everyone. They are all coming in now so I have to go. See you soon."

"I am going over to see Grandma," I said to the kids a few minutes later as they munched sandwiches. "Marie's in charge while I'm away, and I don't want any silly business going on."

"Uh-hah," they nodded.

Hannah picked up her skeleton and Joe fiddled with his lightbulb.

"Put those down Hannah and Joe. Finish eating and do the dishes before you start on your projects again. If you need me for anything, ring Grandma or send someone across the field to get me. I will be back after I have had a cup of tea."

Moments later, I trotted over the paddock past the grazing horses and into my parent's house.

It was relaxing sipping tea in my mother's tidy lounge. I did not need to monitor noises here. I dropped my surveillance radar. Mum's voice and the tick-tock of the clock were soothing. As much as I wanted to prolong the visit, I knew from experience an hour was the longest I could stay. Across the fence in my unsupervised patch, things would be deteriorating. I put my cup down with reluctance and headed back home. Sure enough, as I climbed the wire fence an unholy din greeted me. There was a nasty medley of yelling shrieking and silly laughter.

I stepped through the front door into the main room.

Eating a Light Bulb does not make you Bright

Hannah and Marie were sitting on Joe, while Mark danced about laughing.

"What is going on here?" I thundered.

"Mark has eaten Joe's light bulb and he is going to die," shrieked Marie hysterically.

"What do you mean he has eaten a light bulb? And Hannah, why are you girls sitting on Joe?"

"Joe was going to punch Mark for eating his Christmas tree light. I don't want him to break the glass in Mark's stomach," howled Hannah. "He might die!"

"Serve him right if he does," yelled Joe vindictively, his red face surfacing from under Hannah. "It was a really special lightbulb. Sean gave it to me and now my invention doesn't work anymore!"

"Stop that laughing Mark. You have been a very naughty boy," I said in rising panic. My mind was in a whirl. What do you do when your son has eaten a light bulb? No child-rearing book has a section on that!

"Hannah, has Ambulance training taught you anything about a situation like this?" I asked.

"Well, there was a little girl who swallowed a pin. They fed her cotton-wool sandwiches."

"Cotton-wool sandwiches?" I said mystified.

"The cotton-wool wraps around the sharp object and protects the organs until it passes through the system," said Hannah getting off Joe.

"O.K, grab the first aid kit and get a roll of cotton-wool please Hannah," I commanded. "Marie make a peanut butter sandwich." The things you do as a mother! I thought taking a wad of white fluff from Hannah. I spread it thickly over the peanut butter and gave it to Mark.

"Eat this up," I said to him.

Wendy Hamilton

I pasted happily and the room started to transform.

Eating a Light Bulb does not make you Bright

I braced myself for a fuss, but he woofed it down with gusto. I watched him in astonishment. How could a boy (who gagged over vegetables) eat a light bulb and cotton wool so easily? It was a mystery.

When the crisis was over, I looked around the trashed room. The dishes were not done, the crumbs not swept up, and there was glue, paper, crayons, and Lego blocks spread all over the place.

"I want this all cleaned up and then you can do some schoolwork," I said in a grim tone. There was a general groan.

"No don't moan. When I see behavior like this, I know you need schoolwork. Marie and Hannah, I want you to write a story each."

"I don't know what to write," said Hannah.

"Write about Harriet Tubman then," I said snappily. "Joe get out your math's book and start working through the sums on pages eleven and twelve. If you get stuck come and see me. Mark find your handwriting book. I want a line each of all the alphabet letters. Make them nice and neat and hold your pencil the way I showed you. You can work together in the same room. But if I hear any silly noises, you will all be separated until your father comes home. Do I make myself clear?"

They nodded looking subdued as they sloped off to clean up and find exercise books. I resumed pasting wallpaper onto the wall. I heard the chinks of dishes getting clean and the hum of brains at work. So long as the house sounded like a healthy beehive, I would leave everyone alone. A good learning environment is like tennis; you have to whack the ball from time to time to keep it in the air. Thank goodness I had ears. Sometimes my ears saw more than my eyes.

Wendy Hamilton

Purple Pants

Mark was hard on clothes. It was good he was my last child. Clothes only lasted half a season with my youngest. Any garment unfortunate enough to encounter that boy was on death row. There was never anything to hand down or pass on after Mark. The knees of trousers got the worst hammering. Shortly after meeting Mark, they evaporated into gaping holes. It was as if they saw him coming and hid.

I sighed as I fingered the latest casualties. There was no way around it, I would have to custom design some Mark-proof pants. Reluctantly, I put aside the rag dolls I was making. I preferred sewing dainty little dresses to armor plating a boy. There was one bright spot, however, I needed to buy more fabric.

The next day at my favorite store, I kept my eyes averted from the cotton fabrics with the small print patterns. I needed to stay focused. I was not here for that gorgeous navy blue and burgundy plaid. I needed a heavy strong material that combined warmth and wear. The word SALE written in huge red letters caught my eye. I headed for the table underneath the sign and rummaged through the fabric. There was tulle for tutus, lycra for swimsuits and chiffon for evening dresses. I rubbed a brocade between my fingers speculatively, sighed and dropped it back on the table. Although it was tempting to upholster Mark, Ian would not approve of the floral pattern.

"I need a bit of help here Lord," I prayed. I knew the right fabric was somewhere in the pile. I just hadn't spotted it yet.

Look down. The thought niggled at my mind. I peered beneath the table. Under six bolts of waterproof nylon, I glimpsed a purple corner. I pulled it out.

"Hmmmmmm," almost a full bolt of purple corduroy. I crumpled it in my hands to gauge the thickness and thread density. It was heavy and strong. The color, however, was not quite what I had in mind. I don't think Mark would like it, I thought doubtfully. Still, it was good quality. I searched for the price ticket. Eighteen dollars a meter marked down to two dollars a meter. In the light of this new information, my doubts melted away. Purple was a beautiful color. Mark would love purple pants. Moreover, there was enough to see Mark through to adulthood. I dumped the bolt on top of the counter.

"How many meters?" asked the shop-girl expectantly, her scissors held in readiness.

"All of it," I said decisively.

Back home, I sat my new treasure on top of my stash of fabric.

"What's that for?" asked Ian spotting my purchase. "Let me guess! You've turned Bohemian and you are going to cover the couch with it."

"Don't be cheeky, I am going to turn it into pants for Mark."

Ian snorted. "Does he know yet?"

"Not yet."

"You will have a fight on your hands when he does."

"Oh get out of here! A seven-year-old boy must do what he's told," I said firmly. I pulled a roll of brown paper out of the cupboard and spread it across the floor.

"Mark-proof pants need a wide elastic waist," I mumbled to myself as I made marks on the paper. "And no zip; he forgets to pull it up." I checked his measurements before drawing a swooping line down to the crotch.

"Double stitching at the seams of the seat," I murmured drawing a line of dashes. "That boy could be in a circus his legs are so often twisted up around his ears. Now for the knees." I marked their position on the legs. "Triple layers machine-quilted for extra strength."

When my pattern was finished, I cut out six garments and set them aside. Tomorrow I would zoom them up on my sewing machine provided no one fell off the playhouse roof.

The next day was abnormally trouble free. Contrary to my expectations, nobody fell off the roof and my sewing went without a hitch. Getting my son to wear his customized pants, however, was not so hassle free.

"I'M NOT WEARING THOSE!" Mark was emphatic.

"Yes, you are. You're not wearing those ripped old things any longer. Get them off and try these on." I was equally emphatic, as I handed a new pair of trousers to him.

There was a lot of grumbling and stomping in the bathroom but eventually, Mark appeared with purple legs and a glowering face.

"Haha! Look at Mark, he looks like Mr. Purple-Pants!"

Eating a Light Bulb does not make you Bright

laughed Joe.

Mr. Purple-Pants was a local character. His strange antics both delighted and terrified the kids of the neighborhood. They watched him from behind bushes and sniggered. He was a middle-aged man who strutted around the streets with a strange jerky gait.

"Was he born that way or was he on drugs?"

The question was a source of much junior speculation. He muttered to himself as he strode stiffly about. His rigid posture and swinging arms accentuated his huge beer belly, which preceded the rest of his body for some distance. It was exceedingly unfortunate that he always wore purple pants.

Mark, on hearing Joe's remark, burst into fresh wailing.

"Be quiet Mark. If you carry on like that, I'll fine you two dollars," I said sharply, as I glared at Joe.

"All the kids at music will laugh at me and call me Mr. Purple-Pants," sniveled Mark.

"No, they won't, because if they do, you will tell them that your mother has heaps of purple fabric and that she will make free trousers for all the kids that tease you. And you know those mothers with big families are only too keen to stretch a dollar. Now go and find your recorder, it's time for Youth Music."

A smile broke over Mark's' face.

"Yeah, I'll threaten them with purple pants if anyone dares to say anything."

Youth Music was a blessing. It was held at the Girls High in the evening. For a nominal fee, group tuition could be had in a wide range of instruments. At the end of the year, there was a big concert. Everyone played at the concert from beginners, to a full orchestra, and a Brass Band. Many home-schooling families snapped up the opportunity of cheap music lessons. In the winter when it was too dark for the kids to walk home alone, there were many friends for me to chat to as I waited in the courtyard for my children's classes to finish.

Joe and Mark were in Mrs. Thompson's recorder class. I was fond of the recorder for less than noble reasons; a quality instrument can be purchased for nineteen-ninety-five. When nineteen-ninety-five gets lost, or the car backs over nineteen-ninety-five, it is not too painful.

To Ian's dismay, Marie and Hannah had progressed from the recorder to the violin. Despite their father's rude remarks about yowling cats, the girls heroically persisted in practicing regularly.

Every Friday there was a kerfuffle as the kids hunted for their instruments

"Hurry up boys," shouted Marie as she hauled her violin from the closet. "We mustn't be late. Today is the dress rehearsal for the concert."

There was a stampede as all four of them dashed outside and down the street. A beautiful stillness descended upon the house. I made myself a cup of tea and basked in the peace. I would not get off so lightly on the day of the concert, however. Next Saturday I had to have my brood at the Town Hall by three in the afternoon. At least Mark finally had some tidy pants. If they put him at the back, nobody would see any purple; only the uniform green waistcoat would be visible. The week slipped by. It seemed a few hours ago that I was imagining Mark at the back of the stage. Now it was a reality. I sat in the darkened theater and felt proud. Mark and Joe puffed diligently, their fingers moving in unison with twenty other tootlers. It actually sounded pretty good. In the middle of the performance was a solo item from a more

Eating a Light Bulb does not make you Bright

advanced student. I sat back and relaxed. This was really nice. Suddenly, I sat bolt upright in my seat as a horrible anxiety gripped me. From the back row, a thick streak of purple was rising from the floor. I stared in horror as the purple leg twisted itself up over Mark's shoulder and around the back of his head. My son was obviously bored. A small titter ran around the audience. I wanted to rush onto the stage to stop the dreadful sight. But there was nothing I could do. He was too far away to hiss at or poke with a stick. Disowning him would be the best defense.

"What an odd boy," I said to the stranger beside me. "I bet his mother is very embarrassed right now."

After the performance, I laughed with my friends over Mark's impromptu circus act.

"At least he doesn't suffer from stage fright," said Sharon as we folded waistcoats and packed them in Mrs. Thompson's bag.

"Where are all the kids?" I asked when it was time to go home.

"They're climbing trees in the park," said Mrs. Thompson. "The quickest way to get there is out the back entrance."

A few minutes later I spied Mark. I was pleased to see his pants had survived the rigors of the Botanical Garden. But his sweater! I looked at it in despair. He looked like a street urchin; Oliver Twist had fewer tatters than my son. His top flapped about in shredded rags.

"How did you wreck your jersey?" I asked in horror.

"Don't know!" said Mark looking at his sleeve in surprise.

"He used it to haul himself up the tree," said Marie smugly. "I told him and all the other kids to get down or the Mayor would send them to prison. But they just ignored me," she finished self-righteously.

Sharon smothered a laugh. "This is what happens when a mother spends her time making dolls clothes," she said cheekily.

"The dolls will be on hold until I customize some Mark-proof tops," I said sighing. "Perhaps I could find some orange canvas on sale."

Eating a Light Bulb does not make you Bright

A Modern Problem?

"I wish every day was Christmas," I told my mother in the good-old-days when Christmas meant eating myself sick and Santa coming down the chimney. Back then I couldn't understand her shudder of horror.

"Christmas comes around far too fast," she said emphatically.

I looked at her in disbelief. I did not realize that Christmas for her was shopping, cooking, and expense. Moreover, there was nothing exciting under the tree. At best there might be a lumpy tea cozy or a pair of new slippers.

When I woke up to this sad reality, I realized I needed a new focus for Christmas or I would be miserable. I made the transition from getting to giving, and the new attitude worked a treat. I found pleasure in making Christmas wonderful for my children and people who were alone.

What troubled me now, was the run of activities that blighted the path to the twenty-fifth of December. There were always Christmas parties and barbeques. At least the Christmas parties were one-off events, unlike the rehearsals. There were rehearsals for the Nativity play, the Youth Music concert, carol singing, and the church cantata. It did not help that summer holidays followed Christmas. Summer holidays meant an influx of out-of-town visitors or packing to go out of town yourself. Like my mother, I thought Christmas came around far too fast. It was looming again. The countdown was on and a dark cloud hung over me. I felt exhausted.

"Hurry up or we will be late for music lessons," I shouted irritably.

I found getting anywhere on time very stressful. I tried to keep my life quiet but the pace of modern living was spinning out of control. I waited a few more minutes before tooting the horn. Marie, Joe, and Mark straggled out of the house.

"Where is Hannah?" I hissed at them.

"She is still looking for her violin," said Joe as he buckled up his seat-belt.

I bashed my hand on the horn again.

Hannah looking flustered, rushed out slamming the door behind her.

"Next Wednesday, I expect you to be more organized than this," I said grimly as she climbed into her seat.

I put the van into reverse and started backing out the driveway. I saw Hannah's lips quivering in the rear vision mirror.

"And don't blub," I added nastily.

I felt guilty over the last remark, but I was too tired to fix it. I wonder what I can send Elizabeth this year? I thought as I pulled out into a gap in the traffic. Perhaps a tin of cookies like last year. I can post those. I changed gears as I rounded

Eating a Light Bulb does not make you Bright

a steep corner, my speed dropping to the slow crawl of the huge truck in front of me. It had come from the forestry and was loaded with pine logs. I stared at the pile of lumber on the trailer. The restraining chains looked flimsy compared to the log mass. For a fleeting moment, I savored the mental image of the chains snapping and the logs careering down through my windscreen. The van and my life would be obliterated. The idea seemed pleasant and restful.

A squabble in the back seat flicked me back into reality. If I went, all those with me, died too. Although the mental image was brief, it disturbed me that I could have a suicidal thought. I had experienced burnout when the girls were little and did not want to go down that track again.

I need to carve out more space in my life, I thought as the truck turned down a side road. But how? I put my foot down and the van picked up speed again. Tonight was Ian's work party. Next week was filled with extra choir practices. I had to make costumes for the nativity play between baking and icing a fruit cake. Moreover, the front room needed re-papering and who knew how many visitors I would have popping in over the next few weeks? By the time I pulled into Penny's driveway I was no closer to an answer. At least I could snatch a rest as I waited for the girls to finish their lessons.

Once the music lessons were over, we headed back home. I had a precious half hour before I had to feed the kids and get ready for the babysitter. My eyes glanced idly at a shabby book lying on a small table. I love old books. This one was two-hundred-years old and bound with cords. I picked it up and threw myself into a nearby chair. The pen and ink drawings were plentiful. I leafed through the pages, stopping to linger over an elegant lady driving a carriage. A sentence in the accompanying article caught my eye.

"It is hard to find time for God and rest in this hectic modern pace of living."

Modern!

Shock and illumination shot through me. Modern back then was a crinoline, bonnet and a horse-drawn carriage.

Two hundred years and many advances in technology separated me from this woman, and yet her struggle mirrored mine. In an ah-ha moment, I realized a hectic pace of life is not linked to the twenty-first century, Christmas or technology. What I faced was an ancient problem. Busyness is a spiritual condition.

I fell to my knees.

"Lord forgive me for rushing around being Martha instead of sitting at your feet like Mary. Show me how to cut the rubbish out of my life so I am rested and have time to listen to you."

Little by little as I sat there, it became clear what I must do. The front room could stay shabby and the girls would not be taking violin lessons next term. They could keep going to youth Music because they could walk there. From now on we would not participate in anything that needed rehearsals or costumes. I could buy an iced fruit cake and we should avoid going away over Christmas time.

I rang my sister-in-law.

"Hi Elizabeth, let's just swap Christmas cards and forget the presents. It's too much work, especially as our kids are past the coloring-in-book stage," I suggested.

"That would be good, you can buy yourself a tin of biscuits from me," Ian's sister joked sounding relieved.

That was ten years ago. The future is the now. I have more technology in the house than ever before. Life is very modern; just as it was in the recent twentieth century and the not so recent seventeenth and eighteenth century. Yet amidst all the huffing and puffing of this world, my life cruises along leisurely. I have uneventful days that meander. There is time to smell the roses, pat the cat and drink tea on the veranda. I seldom go out, but when I do, it's for something important like a doctor's appointment or hobbies. I have time to quilt, sew, paint, write, garden and even run a shop in my house. My home is filled with industry but not busyness. The kids and I beaver away on projects that we love. We are productive but not driven. There is time for a chat with the neighbor or the occasional visitor. We don't rush around and treasure our uncluttered lifestyle.

In her room, Marie writes a novel. In the attic Joe composes music. There is a knock on my bedroom door.

"Come in," I call as I put aside my own scribbling. It is Mark.

"Look at my latest drawing Mum."

He shows me a sketch and I am impressed. For a boy who has only drawn four pencil pictures in his life, it is marvelously good. Usually, he is more interested in computer animation and draws by dragging and clicking his mouse.

"I want to get a more realistic look to my characters," he tells me. "I think if I started sketching it would help."

We examine his drawing together and agree the eyes are a little high.

"Next time I'll do them closer to the middle of the head," he says.

"Did you try modeling with the clay I bought you yesterday?" I ask.

"Yes, but it is a bit sticky, I need some modeling tools."

I make a mental note to see if the hobby shop sells them

next time I am in town. I look around the nicely decorated room. Slowing up did not mean I did nothing. It just meant taking a little longer to do things and being more selective over activities. Time like money is not limitless. You need to be prayerful and wise about how you spend it. Hectic living is not a modern problem. It started with Adam and Eve eating the forbidden fruit, and is a horrible way to live.

Eating a Light Bulb does not make you Bright

It is a Marathon Not a Sprint

I'm not keen on ladies camps. They have too many lectures and not enough fun for my taste. This one for home-schooling mums, however, sounded promising. It had a reputation for pampering women. I liked the sound of that. Pampering and no cooking had definite appeal. Besides, a lot of my friends were going.

"Wahoo," I said as I threw my luggage into the back of Sharon's van. "No kids for a whole weekend!"

"It's going to be a squeeze," said Sharon.

"I don't care," I said sitting next to my friend Janine. "This is going to be a great weekend. I have packed the essentials; chocolate and a good book."

All eight women laughed. It did not take much to make us laugh. We were riding high on childlessness. The wheels of the van spun as we joked. The further we got from our homes, the funnier the kids seemed; grim lines around mouths softened and furrowed brows smoothed. After four-hundred-miles, toddlers and tantrums seemed hilarious; especially when we thought of our husbands dealing with them.

It was dark when we arrived at the camp.

The large lobby when we entered swarmed with women. By the registration, was a pile of pink paper bags with twine handles. They looked tantalizingly interesting. My group lined up to sign in.

"Write your name," said a woman with short hair and a ski jacket. She handed me a marker pen and pointed to a roll of hello-my-name-is, stickers. In the blank space, I wrote WENDY and stuck it on my chest.

"We have a gift bag for each of you lovely ladies," said the woman next to her. Her large earrings wobbled as she handed me a pink bag.

"Thank you……..?" I took a quick glance at her chest. "Thank you, Annabel."

"You're welcome. We have assigned your group cabin D7. I hope you have had your dinner already. There's a light supper, but that is all."

I nodded that we had, thinking of the stop for Chinese Take-aways.

"Good," she said acknowledging my nods. "Breakfast is at seven thirty in the morning and this evening's meeting starts in half an hour," she continued, "cabins are through there." She pointed to a door under an EXIT sign. "Get settled in and have a great time," she finished kindly as she handed me a blue pamphlet.

I stuffed my pillow into the crook of my arm and picked up my case before shuffling to the side. My sleeping bag slipped and I hitched the string back over my shoulder.

Eating a Light Bulb does not make you Bright

"D7 is down here," said Sharon leading the way.

She had been here before. I and the others followed her down a long veranda lined with many doors. Our cumbersome bags banged against our legs as we walked. A baby cried. Babies were the only children allowed.

"I'm glad none of us have a baby," I muttered to Janine. "I hope it's not in the room next to us."

"Here we are," said Sharon opening a door.

The room was basic. It was made of white concrete blocks and furnished with ten wooden bunks. All of my friends hoisted their bags onto a top bunk and threw their sleeping gear onto the bed below. I, however, dumped my pillow on a top bunk. I had not outgrown the pleasure of sleeping up high. Still clutching the pamphlet, I spread out my sleeping bag and hoofed myself up onto it. It felt good to lie down after our long trip. I smoothed out the blue paper.

"Wow! Have you seen this program? There is no way I'm going to all that!"

My Friends just laughed. They were used to me and not surprised by my outburst.

"Why not Wendy?" teased Sharon. "I thought you would love to hear all about reading curriculums and learning styles."

"Yes, ten years ago," I snorted. "It's pretty boring now."

"I've been at this twenty years but I'm still going to all the lectures," said Sharon.

"That's because you are a saint. Any woman who home-school's ten children is a saint. Why don't you eat chocolate instead of going to the meetings, like me?" I tempted her.

"I don't want to get fat," said Sharon.

I snorted. Sharon was tall and looked like a model. "You won't get fat."

"Maybe not, but I don't want to miss Violet Blast. She is the keynote speaker this year," she added slyly.

"Well I wouldn't want to deny you a pleasure like that," I said throwing my pillow at her.

The next morning after a wonderful breakfast, I had the bunkroom and the campgrounds all to myself. The silence was an unspeakable luxury. I sat on my bed and went through my pink bag at leisure. I felt like a kid on Christmas morning as I inspected each article thoroughly. There were skin care products, a nice scented soap, a nail brush, a bookmark, four Belgium chocolates, and lots of pamphlets. I sucked a chocolate slowly as I read through the pamphlets. It seemed only fair to read the advertising in exchange for the goodies.

After two chocolates, I knew all about the hydrating wonders of my sample moisturizes. After three chocolates, how they would benefit my aging skin. At the end of four chocolates, it was morning tea time. I heard the sound of women chattering as they moved from the main hall to the dining room. I jumped down and joined the throng. I was very interested in this part of the program.

As I stirred milk into my tea and picked up a scone, a young woman caught my eye. She sat slumped in a chair at a table in the corner. She looked very tired; too tired in fact to savor the raspberry and cream on her scone. Beside her was a baby in a stroller.

I bet she has several children and is trying too hard, I thought. She looks like she would be better off spending the weekend, like me; lazing about.

Janine waved to me from a nearby table.

"Are you having a nice time?" she asked as I put my cup on the table.

"Lovely this is a real break."

Eating a Light Bulb does not make you Bright

Sharon slid into the seat beside me. "Are you going to the next lecture Wendy?" she asked looking at me slyly. "I'm sure you would get a lot out of it."

"Oh really?"

"It's Violet Blast speaking on family devotions," she said wickedly.

"Oh I don't think so, but don't let me stop you benefiting from Violet's wisdom!" I said demurely.

I was the last to leave the dining room. The kitchen staff were rinsing dishes and the women were in the hall listening to Violet when I left. Back in the bunkroom, I took out a book and read a few pages before throwing it down. No, I did not feel like reading.

I suppose Violet is flattening everyone as usual I thought. Since the days of the bread portfolio, I had seen it many times. Violet portrayed her life as heaven come to earth. Young women listened to her in awe and crumpled under the unrealistic bar she set.

To get my mind off Violet, I decided to finish a quilt block. For me, craft was the ultimate relaxation.

I pulled a square of cream fabric from my bag. On it was the image of a small cottage; outlined in a continuous line of red stitches. All it needed was a bit of strategic staining to finish it off.

Now, where was my artist's brush? Big handbags are a nightmare to find anything in, I thought, as I rummaged in its dark inside. The multiple zips did not help. Eventually, I found my brush; right at the bottom. Now all I needed was some black tea.

The dining room was shut when I scooted back. No hope of getting a tea bag there! I remembered the Overflow Room next to the main hall. It was set aside for the women nursing babies. There was a big screen in there, and more importantly, a kitchenette. I bet I could get hot water and a couple of tea bags there. Unfortunately, it meant exposure to Violet's fairy tale. I resisted as long as I could, but the urge to do something creative was compelling. I let myself in quietly through the side door. Good, I saw coffee and tea bags stacked neatly in containers on the bench. I sidled around the comfortable couches scattered about the room. The room had a homely lounge-like feel to it. It was infinitely more pleasant than the bunkroom. Perhaps I could avoid looking at Violet. I made two cups of tea and slid them onto a coffee table before sinking into a couch my back towards the screen. Opposite me sat the young woman I had noticed at morning tea.

I could ignore Violet's gigantic head but I could not block out her voice. Her melodious voice filled the room as I drank tea from one cup and stained fabric with the other.

"And in the morning," said the big mouth, "I gather my precious chickens around me as we open up the word of God and just enjooooooooooy a time of fellowship together. Then we pray for an hour. It is sooooooo important to have family devotions every day, after all, the family that prays together stays together."

I saw the woman opposite me wilt. She clutched her baby close and slumped lower in her seat. I expect it was the hour of prayer that unraveled her. I ground my teeth as I thought of our own hideous little family devotions. Fortunately, they were spasmodic. Unlike Violet's perfect family, the imperfect Hamilton family did not enjoooooooooooy devotional times. I sincerely doubted the authenticity of Violets assertions. People are people, kids are kids and life dishes out mountains and valleys to everyone. There had to be a lot of massaging of the truth in Violet's presentation. Unfortunately, the young woman opposite me believed the propaganda. I could tell by her face as flashes of grim determination struggled with shadows of defeat.

I wanted to lean forward and say, "hey when it gets difficult don't try harder, get worse, and do less. If you don't get reading done this week and little Mark is slow at math's, don't sweat it. The years will know what the days will never know. Don't beat yourself up when family devotions collapse. That is not the best way to pass on faith anyway. There is a much easier way to go about this. You don't have to copy churches, schools, or the superwoman on the screen."

But instead, I silently stained my cottage brown, as Violet exhorted us to shoot for perfection.

At the end of the session, everyone except the woman opposite me filed out. I caught her eye.

"It's so hard!" she blurted out. "I want to home-school my children but I keep failing. I tried with my son a few years ago but I didn't think I was doing a good enough job, so I put him into school. I took him out again because he hated it, and got bullied. I want to keep him at home but I am on the brink of sending him back. I just don't think I can do it," she ended, tears trickling down her face.

I moved into the seat beside her and patted her shoulder.

"I've been doing this for over fifteen years. Nobody has been as lax as me but my kids are coming out fine," I comforted her. "I'll tell you a secret I learned many years ago. Home-schooling is a marathon, not a sprint. When the pain kicks in, don't stop, slow down. You can't turn your home into an institutional school. The institutional methods will burn you out. Just be a warm mum and create an interesting learning environment. You will find the job gets done without you knowing how it happened. Let me tell you about my column cashbook method……….."

As I spoke, I could see relief and hope rising in her. The bell rang for lunch.

"Oh, just one more piece of advice, if I were you I wouldn't go to all the lectures. Now is a chance to catch up on sleep. Or if you feel up to it, there is a short bush walk over by the playground."

She laughed as together we sauntered over to the dining room.

One day I thought, as I ate lasagna, I am going to write a book for exhausted home-schooling mums. Someone needs to tell them about the messy reality of a good home-school.

Eating a Light Bulb does not make you Bright

Unexpected Blooms

"Thank you for inviting us to watch your house arrive," I said to Susie who lived at the end of our road.

"Nice of you to come and take an interest" she replied. "I think the five AM start has put everyone else off.".

"I wouldn't have missed it for anything," I said. "It brings back memories of when we shifted the second building onto our property, it was small, however, and fitted on one truck, this is the first time I've seen them join two halves together. It's very exciting."

"Yes it is exciting," agreed Susie.

"I just love old Kauri Villas. It is going to be really something when you have done it all up."

"I hope so," replied Suzie modestly. "I've always wanted to have a go at Bed and Breakfast."

"Well, it will certainly be big enough for that once the new building is joined to your house. And the views, spectacular of course! With any luck, you'll get a lot of Germans. Germans love this area."

We talked as we watched the men at work in the dim light. Bit by bit as the sun crept over the horizon they maneuvered the house into position. The motor that powered the hydraulic arms throbbed and whined as they tilted the house about. It was tricky lining up two halves and one existing building; especially as everything had to be level.

"Joe, don't get too close and don't get in the men's way," I admonished Joe. He had been inching closer and closer to the truck, fascinated by the whole process. I drew a line in the dirt with a stick.

"Don't go over this line!"

"O.K. Mum," he said squatting down.

Little by little, we watched the two halves become a house again. We held our breath as the trucks started to inch out from underneath the temporary supports and cheered when they got out safely. The post-hole borers (drilling into the ground like giant screws) were wonderful lunchtime entertainment. As were the foundation piles and the revolving belly of the concrete truck later in the day.

It was dark by the time the house was finally lowered into its new position. As we drove home everyone agreed that it had been a fabulous day. Despite this, I was troubled.

"Another day hits the dirt," I moaned to Ian when the kids were in bed. "We haven't done a lick of schoolwork today."

"Never mind," he said, "tomorrow is another day."

"Tomorrow will be a write off too," I said morosely. "What is it about housework and laundry that if you miss a day it takes the whole week to catch up again?"

"That is one of the great mysteries of life," said Ian taking a sip of tea.

I chewed the end of a pencil and gazed at the columns

in my cash books. Could I legitimately fill out any blank spaces other than socialization?

"Do you think reading 'Harold's House Movers' off the side of the cab qualifies as reading?" I asked him, my pencil hovering over the Reading column.

"It's stretching the truth a bit. But it doesn't really matter."

I sighed. He was right of course, on both points. "At least I can fill in the technology box," I said brightening as a thought hit me. "The day has been technology from beginning to end."

I scribbled down some notes and slammed the book shut. It had been a long day and I was tired.

The next morning dawned bright and sunny. As predicted, I did not listen to the enthralling antics of Janet and Mark and their jumping dog Tip. Hearing Mark read was less important than Ian's dirty socks.

"You kids can occupy yourselves today," I said after the dishes were done and the beds made. I'm busy. If I hear any silly twaddle or fighting, however, I will set you some schoolwork."

At this everyone scattered. I heard Joe rummaging in the back shed for tins and junk as I loaded the washing machine. I pulled out the ON knob and water trickled into the big bowl.

I loved the spring water of our country property but the water pressure was pathetic. It took ages to run through a wash cycle. Eventually, however, it was done. As I pegged washing onto the clothesline, I could see Joe tinkering about on the veranda.

Wendy Hamilton

"Joe, don't get too close."

Eating a Light Bulb does not make you Bright

The girls were grooming their horses and Mark was riding his bike up and down the driveway. It was pleasant and I felt happy as I carried the empty washing basket back to the laundry room.

"Mum, come and look at the hydraulic lift I've made," said Joe coming up behind me.

"You've made a hydraulic lift?" My mind boggled. I did not know he knew the word hydraulic. I was only vaguely aware of it myself. Hydro; something to do with water I suppose.

I followed him feeling curious. Scattered over the ground was the normal medley of junk I associated with my eldest son. He was always pulling apart old computers, small motors and anything with wires. He had purloined my embroidery box and filled the compartments with nuts, bolts, and nameless electronic pieces. Right now he was fiddling with a couple of empty cans; one of which was slotted into the other. A small hose ran from the outside can and into a bucket of water.

"See, if I pump water between the cans, the inside one will lift up," he explained. There was a small buzzing sound as he flicked a switch and the inside-can rose just as he predicted.

"It leaks a bit but all hydraulics leak," he added matter-of-factly.

"How did you learn all this stuff?" I asked in astonishment. He certainly had not learned this from me!

"Oh, watching the trucks yesterday and I just sort of know it," he finished vaguely.

"This is absolutely marvelous," I said feeling delighted that there was something magnificent to put in Joe's column cash book. Through the haze of euphoria, a small concern niggled at me. Something was missing. It was the sound of running water. I looked over at the half-barrel in the garden. Water should have been trickling out of the old-fashioned hand-pump.

"Why is my fountain not working?" I asked Joe suspiciously.

"I borrowed it for my hydraulics," he said sheepishly.

"Well make sure you put it back when you have finished," I said torn between delight and annoyance.

I turned around and noticed something else was missing.

"What have you done with my bench seat?" I asked.

"That wasn't me," he said quickly. "The girls took it.

I could hear a commotion coming from the paddock behind the big trees.

"What did they want it for?"

"I don't know. They said they needed it for an experiment."

I looked at Joe playing with his hydraulic lift and my spirits rose. I wonder what the girls have invented while I've been wrestling with dirty undies? I thought. Full of anticipation I went to investigate.

Eating a Light Bulb does not make you Bright

Mark

"Spell love, Mark."

"L-a-v-e. "

Ahhh! Inwardly I tore my hair. "0, not A, Mark!"

How many times did we have to go over this? Mark was eleven, spoke with a lisp, and still not reading or writing. Every book I read on Dyslexia, described Mark perfectly. It was hardly surprising; Dyslexia ran in the family. It was comforting in a dark way, that school was no more successful at teaching Mark's cousin than, I was at teaching Mark.

"Put your spelling books away," I said wearily.

He wandered off, and I heard the thump of the cupboard door as he slung them into the hutch-dresser. All too soon, he was back.

"When I grow up, I'm going to own a Lego factory," he said.

"Hmm, that's nice," I said mechanically. I did not think I could stand a whole morning of Mark following me around yapping about Lego. Lego blocks were his one and only interest (if you did not count talking). The whole family was sick of hearing about Lego, and I was sick of millions of tiny blocks spread over the lounge floor. I looked at the rain dribbling down the windowpane and sighed. Unfortunately, sending him outside was not an option.

If Mark was my first child, I probably would have given up on homeschooling, convinced I was a total failure as a teacher.

Marie had had trouble learning to read, her struggles, however, were small compared to Mark's difficulties.

"What do I do about this child, Lord?" I prayed. "He needs more interests and his mind has to be stretched, but I don't know how to do it."

"Creativity springs from boredom." The words dropped into my mind. "Remember Marie's first picture?"

I certainly did.

It is time Mark drew something, I thought, seizing a pencil and paper.

"Can I have a Lego spaceship for Christmas?" asked Mark treading on the back of my heel as he trailed behind me.

"Ouch, I want you to go into my room," I said, cutting him short, "and draw me a picture. You can take a book with you but it has to be one with only words in it."

"How long do I have to stay there?" he asked, his mouth drooping.

"All morning."

"Ahh, all morning," wailed Mark, "by myself?"

"By yourself," I said firmly. "You can come out at 10 o'clock for a morning tea break." I handed him the paper and pencil. He took them as if they were a bomb about to explode and stamped off. Just before the door slammed, I heard him muttering darkly about the horrors of the 'Solitude of Solitudes.'

Determined to make the most of my reprieve, I packed away all the Lego blocks, made myself a cup of tea and enjoyed my tidy lounge.

The morning passed swiftly. All too soon it was 10 o clock. I dawdled down the hallway and let him out as promised.

"What did you draw?" I asked. As he had never drawn a picture before, I had little hope of anything beyond a few squiggles.

He handed me a picture of an animal that looked remarkably like an anteater. "Wow, Mark, this is amazing," I said, genuinely shocked. "You're an artist."

"Nah, not really," said Mark.

"That's really good, Mark," said Joe, coming up and looking at Mark's work. "You should get into 3D modeling. I'll show you how to find tutorials on modeling with Blender if you like?"

"Can I Mum, or do I have to go back to the Solitude of solitude?"

"No, you can do that instead," I said beaming.

That was the start of Mark's love affair with the computer. He began by modeling a simple cube that he learned to turn into chairs, and tables, rocks, and trees, even eventually, animated characters.

I bought home thick textbooks from the library on the subject. As the books were far above his low reading level, I read them aloud to him.

"Is this making sense to you?" I asked after reading page after page of incomprehensible gobble-dee-gook.

"Yeah, yeah."

"Ok, I'll carry on then," I said, starting to read again.

When I finished the chapter, he rushed off to try what he had learned.

I smiled as I closed the heavy book. Mark's spelling looked like Swahili, and his reading was abysmal; with God's help, however, we had stumbled across something he excelled in.

Eating a Light Bulb does not make you Bright

More Propaganda

It was a beautiful spring morning on Mount Tiger. A feeling of great wellbeing engulfed me as I sat on the veranda of the top building. The sun-kissed the roses that climbed up the veranda posts and hung from the spouting in pink clusters. The bricks under my feet were warm. A bumblebee meandered in and out of daffodils in the nearby garden. Meanwhile, honey bees buzzed around the lavender. The cat brushed against my leg. I picked him up and put him on my knee.

"Oh no you don't," I said blocking him with my hand as he stretched his nose forward. "You don't need to sniff my cup; coffee is not for cats.".

On the grassy patch in front of the bottom building, the girls pottered about taking care of their ponies. I could see the boys behind a side wall. Mark carried a reel of electric fence tape while Joe stuck fence standards into the ground. The distance between us muted their voices pleasantly.

"I don't know how Oscar gets so dirty," said Marie

brushing dried mud out of his coat.

"Yeah, they are filthy and as soon as we let them go they will roll in the dirt again," agreed Hannah pulling the horse-cover off Chris. She hung it over the post and rail fence, not far from the boys.

"How does the girl-trap work?" asked Mark loudly.

"Shhh, keep your voice down," said Joe. "We don't want the girls to know about it. Pull the line out a bit we want a big booby trap."

Life doesn't get better than this, I thought as I took a sip of coffee.

On the outdoor table beside me was a stack of magazines. I pulled one out at random. Unfortunately, it was a home-schooling one. Like a thick cloud passing in front of the sun, the cover picture swept my happiness away. Eight kids in order of age sat at a large kitchen table. Their heads (like the treads of a staircase) bent studiously over neat workbooks. They were dressed in blue and white formal clothes and smiled with the perfect teeth of Americans. The Mum bothered me the most. She looked like a fashion model. Her angelic face oozed the patience of Mother Teresa as she lent between two children. Her hand rested lightly on the shoulder of the small boy she was gently instructing; her sharp pencil poised beneath a complex sum of algebra. She favored us briefly with a glowing smile that radiated the joy of teaching, which the cameraman (a skilled wildlife photographer) captured seconds before she returned to her task. I could not imagine her yelling as I regularly did, "what do you mean you left all the school books in town? Last week you told me you couldn't do math's because those books were all out here!"

And certainly, none of those eight saintly kids would have

Eating a Light Bulb does not make you Bright

eaten their brother's light bulb or spend the whole morning making a booby trap for their sisters. I flopped opened the magazine and the perfect family fell face down onto the table top. Inside was another photo. Once again, the children were lined up from the oldest to the youngest. This time each one of them held a violin; even the toddler. An in-depth article gave a résumé of each child's accomplishments. Not only did the four eldest children play in the Denver Symphony Orchestra, but they had also made their violins during their craft lessons. The gray cloud that the cover induced, turned black.

A scream rent the air interrupting my morose thoughts. Joe had electrocuted himself as he tried out his girl trap. It appeared the modifications were not going too well as there had been many similar outbursts.

"I think you boys need to stop playing with the electric fence, you're hurting yourselves too much."

"Oh no please don't make us stop Mum," they begged. "It's sooooooo much fun."

I sighed. While the whole idea seemed foolish and unpleasant to me, the current was not strong enough to be dangerous.

"Well alright, just remember if you touch each other you'll both get zapped. If you put on rubber gumboots, you will stop getting electrocuted because you will be insulated from the current."

"Mum, can you come and help with Oscar?" We are having trouble getting the worm-paste down him," called Marie. She hung grimly onto her pony's bridle as he pranced around rolling his eyes.

"The pamphlet says its apple flavor," said Hannah "but the horses don't believe it."

I slammed the magazine shut and got up, pleased to escape from the Perfect-Family. My girls in jeans and sweatshirts did not look smart like their blue and white peers from across the ocean. They were covered with horse hair, saddle grime, and white streaks of rejected worm paste.

"It's taken us all morning to get Oscar and Chris clean and I know as soon as we let them go they will rush straight back to that muddy patch and roll." Marie stared up at the gathering rain clouds. "By the time we have them wormed I think it will be too wet to go for a ride," she moaned. "I really love Oscar but sometimes I find him a big pain!"

"Get used to it Marie," I said as another burst of bawling broke out from the direction of the girl booby trap. "When you are a mother you will feel like that a lot."

As Marie predicted, the rain had started by the time we got the horses wormed. We let them go and ran for shelter. Once inside, I put a stew on the woodstove to simmer and popped a loaf of bread into the oven. From behind closed doors, sounds of sawing and yowling cats wafted out as the girls played their Made-in-Taiwan violins. No symphony orchestra wanted Marie and Hannah to perform. In fact, Ian had restricted music practice to the hours he was outside the home, claiming it was injurious to his health.

As dinner cooked and the boys played with blocks, the magazine family bothered me again. I did not think I could gather all my kids around the table for anything other than eating. I was not a model, and I did not have the patience of Mother Teresa. I could however at least do a bit of schoolwork with one child.

"Joe come and sit up here. Do you think you could draw me a diagram of a circuit board?"

"Yeah," he responded reluctantly. He wanted to carry on

Eating a Light Bulb does not make you Bright

playing.

"Just leave that for a moment and draw me one, I said putting paper and a stubby pencil on the table. I thought about leaning over him and lying an encouraging hand on his shoulder as he worked but the idea seemed phony. Instead, I busied myself with the fire. Earlier I had written 'experimented with electricity' in the science box of the boy's column cash books, but I felt a bit dishonest about it. It seemed a stretch of the truth to claim that a girl-booby-trap (which zapped boys) was science. I opened the heavy oven door and the latch fell with a dull clank. The bread looked golden and had a nice hollow sound when I tapped it. I tipped it out of the tin and onto the cooling rack above the stove. Its fragrance mingled with the simmering stew and my sense of wellbeing rose sharply. There was something so delightful in this simple little-house-on-the-prairie lifestyle. Handmade bread cooked with fire, made me feel clever and boosted my endorphins. Tomorrow we would go back to town and all the conveniences of modern living. I would enjoy my dishwasher, electricity, and the easy walk to the city center. The seesaw between old and new ways of living was fun.

"Here you go Mum," Joe interrupted my train of thought as he handed me his drawing. "A circuit board was too easy, so I drew you a diagram of a power station." He handed me a complex drawing and my eyes nearly popped out of my head. He knew a lot more about electricity than I did.

It occurred to me as I stuck Joe's diagram on the fridge, that every country has its Violet Blast. I am sure that under the perfect pose of the cover family, there is a less than perfect reality. It is possible that number four and five child fight and call each other adopted zombies. That the baby eats large slugs found under the cat's plate. That it took all morning to get everybody clean and assembled for the photo shoot. That afterward, the Mum slumped and said, "I'm glad that is over," while the toddler washed her doll's hair in the toilet. This is the messy reality of home-schooling where (happily) learning goes on despite everything. And if like horses you don't believe the propaganda on pamphlets, life doesn't get better than a sunny morning, coffee, ponies, and an electric fence.

Eating a Light Bulb does not make you Bright

Digging for Victory

There was a strange voice in the house. It was male and sounded aggressive. I moved quickly towards the noise. It was my fifteen-year-old son. His change in voice had caught me by surprise again. It happened several times a day. Overnight my uncomplicated little boy was gone. In his place was a lanky hobbledehoy; half-man-half-boy.

Right now, the hobbledehoy was shouting at his younger brother. I stomped down the hallway to intervene.

"Joe, bring in the firewood please," I said with authority in my voice.

"That's not fair, why doesn't Mark get the firewood?" He glowered at me through lowered eyebrows.

"Because you're the one I heard shouting and arguing."

"Well, he was arguing too. Why should I do it?"

"Because I am your mother and I told you to. Anyone with that much energy needs more work. If you continue arguing with me, you can peel all the potatoes for dinner as well."

"Work! That's your cure for everything."

"That's right. Mr. Williams says boys are like mules; if you don't work them, you get trouble."

"I am not a mule. Mr. Williams doesn't know what he is talking about."

I looked at his stubborn mulish expression. Technically he was right, a hobbledehoy is not an animal. There are, however, undeniable similarities between them.

"That may be, but it doesn't alter that I want you to bring in the firewood. The basket is empty. As you have the most energy I want you to do it."

"Whatever," he shrugged belligerently as he slouched out the door.

I sighed. Testosterone had changed the game. The days of blocks and small cars were gone. Now it was all about the computer.

"Thank you, Joe," I said when the basket was full.

"Next I would like you to chop some kindling for tomorrow."

"Why can't someone else do it? I want to go back to my computer."

"You are not going back on your computer this afternoon."

"Why not?"

"I let you work on your computer this morning and now you are argumentative and stroppy.

"I am not!"

"I'm not going to argue with you. I want you to go and chop the kindling now."

He stomped off in a huff.

It was always the same. If I let him on the computer in the morning, he became argumentative and full of anger by the afternoon. But if he had two or three hours of manual labor before going on the computer, he kept a sweet and helpful disposition. I looked around the town yard. The fence was painted, the garden weeded, and the trees pruned. I was running out of jobs.

"I'm at my wits end with Joe," I said to Ian later that night. "He needs a paper run or some sort of physical activity to run off the excess energy. If he was the sporty type that would help."

"Yeah, but he is totally uninterested in rugby or soccer," said Ian.

"That wouldn't work for us anyway," I said. "A job or a team sport involves commitment, and our lifestyle of shifting house every few days interferes with that."

"There are plenty of things he could do at Mount Tiger," said Ian thoughtfully. "He could trap and skin possums. There's a big demand for skins at the moment."

"You're right," I said thoughtfully. "And I could get him fencing, gardening, planting trees and landscaping. The cottage is very comfortable now. We could shift there permanently."

"Yes, we could," said Ian getting excited, "and we could rent out the house in town."

"Of course, he will fuss about the work," I said thinking of the fight involved.

"Not if we paid him," said Ian. "He can work in the morning and do his schoolwork in the afternoon."

"That's another thing. He is fifteen. His reading is not fluent, his spelling is horrible, and he is way behind in math's," I said gloomily. "And what about exams? Other kids his age are studying for High School exams. What are we going to do?"

"Don't worry about exams, there are always backdoors," said Ian confidently. "And remember the statistics; home-schoolers often trail behind their peers until the late teens and then they rocket ahead. There is nothing wrong with that boy's brain he is just a late bloomer."

"That's true," I agreed. "I bet none of your teachers would have guessed that you would end up with two Masters Degrees."

"Yeah, I didn't look promising and I still can't spell."

It was not a big job to put our plan into action. Before long we were living permanently at Mount Tiger.

Once the upheaval of the shift was over, I assigned Joe his first job.

"This morning I want you to dig a hole at every place I mark," I said as I strode along a string line dropping a stone every two meters. "The holes need to be this wide," I cut a square of turf, "and at least as deep as the length of your spade. If you hit a rock, use this pick or a wrecking bar to smash it up or lever it out. You can have half an hour's morning tea break at ten o'clock, and make sure you keep your sun hat on. If you work well I will pay you ten dollars."

Joe's eyes sparkled.

"Ten dollars! That's a fortune. I could buy the music software I want and update my computer!"

"Yes you could, and you can have the back shed for a music studio if you like. I'll find you a table and chair and you can set up your sound equipment this afternoon."

He was keen and eager to work. By lunchtime, three sturdy posts stood in a line. I tried to wobble them but they stood firm.

"You have done a really good job Joe," I said handing him a ten dollar note. "Thanks," he said smiling.

Eating a Light Bulb does not make you Bright

Joe did manual labour every morning.

Within a few weeks, he had built a long post and rail fence.

"Now I want you to paint it," I said pointing to a bucket of olive-green paint. "Give it three coats."

He nodded and pushed the earplugs of his phone into his ears. The fence darkened as he steadily worked his way along it.

"Time to finish," I called at mid-day. "Make sure you wash out the paintbrush properly.

"Working is fun when you get paid for it," he said when he came in. "When you do a good job, it makes you feel quite good."

"It sure does."

"What do you want me to do when I have finished the fence?"

"It will take you all week to get three coats on it," I said thinking hard. "Perhaps you could cut a pathway to the bush hut next. You could build steps down the steepest bit. You are good at that sort of thing. Remember all those tracks you and Mark made down by the water tank?"

He nodded. "We did those just for fun. Being paid for it will be even better."

"There is plenty of lumber under the house you can use for the steps."

"Can I start on it tomorrow?"

"No, you need to finish the fence first."

"Then I am going to work extra hard."

"Come and have some lunch," I said handing him a plate of sandwiches.

It was my custom to read aloud a book after lunch. When I had finished reading, Joe rummaged around in the oak cabinet where I kept the schoolwork books.

Eating a Light Bulb does not make you Bright

"Where's the blue math's book Mum?" he asked.

"It's there, look in the middle cupboard. What do you want it for?" I asked curiously. The sight of Joe searching for a textbook voluntarily seemed strange.

"I have realized Mum that you are a useless teacher. I need to teach myself."

"You are absolutely right Joe. You only retain thirty percent of things others teach you. But if you discover it for yourself, you remember seventy percent. I am here if you need help. And if I can't figure it out Dad will know or you can Google it."

"Thanks, Mum," he said as he opened the thick book.

For two years Joe did manual labor every morning. In the afternoon he educated himself, and composed music. When he was seventeen he was accepted for Community College with no High School qualifications. He studied diligently and was a straight-A student. Best of all he was not swayed by his peers as he had his own identity. He made friends easily but was not led into the party-culture that many of them were involved in.

One day Joe came home with astonishing news.

"Mum, do you want to hear the biggest joke ever?"

"Of course," I said thinking he had another knock-knock joke.

"My teacher said that you must be an outstanding teacher because I was so well educated!"

At this, the entire family roared with laughter.

"I don't know what you are all finding so funny," I said trying to keep a straight face. "None of you would be able to use a computer if I hadn't taught you."

At this, there was another burst of laughter.

"Yeah right," said Mark sarcastically, "you don't even

know how to print out something."

"That's nothing," said Hannah, "yesterday she couldn't remember how to turn on her laptop."

As I write this, Marie is twenty-four an author and an illustrator. She is almost fluent at reading Latin (a language I know nothing about). She teaches English as a second language and is interested in political science and history. It astonishes me that the kid with the big mouth who drove me crazy has turned into this elegant young woman. The endless drivel about centipede legs has metamorphosed into eloquent ideas. I enjoy her original thinking and spiritual depth.

Hannah, my quiet slow-to-warm-up child. Who would have thought she was capable of flying alone to Dubai to join the mercy-ship The Logos Hope? That the girl who dissolved into tears if a stranger looked at her, could look after orphans in Sri Lanka and clean deep wells in a war-torn country. She was the first of us to publish a book. Her book Hidden Struggles is written to help young women through the difficult teen years.

There is a rich sound of an orchestra pulsing through the house. It sounds like a movie score. It is not coming from the CD player, it is one of Joe's original compositions. Our nineteen-year-old son is a fine young man who is making good life-choices. On his own initiative, he traded in the garden spade to work voluntarily at the Salvation Army. He is about to go off to Bible College before he decides what career to pursue.

Mark at sixteen is still fumbling around and not impressive in the three Rs. Sometimes I am tempted to panic over his spelling. When I do, Ian reminds me that all of our children are late bloomers, but when the fruit eventually

Eating a Light Bulb does not make you Bright

ripens, it is good. There are signs of buds about to blossom in Mark. He is talented with the computer his character is shaping up well and the other day he told me that I was a useless teacher.

My advice to a nervous home-schooling mum is this; make your home a warm interesting place. Focus on character training rather than academics. Somehow, despite your bumbling inefficiency, your children will be educated by twenty; just as they learned to speak a language without you putting much effort into it.

The most important thing of all, however, is to pray daily for wisdom. The God who made a boy's lunch feed a crowd, and knows the future, is abundantly able to multiply your feeble efforts into a wonderful education for your children.

Wendy Hamilton

Prologue - University

We shifted to Australia, and at age twenty, Joe entered Western Sydney University and did a diploma in Engineering, which gave him the first year of his Bachelor of Electrical engineering. He is currently in his final year and doing very well. He is a straight-A student, has a near perfect GPA and has made the Dean's Merit list for the last three years. He is set to graduate at the end of 2019.

Mark was a very late bloomer. At age eighteen he was finally ready for formal education. He entered Tafe (Community College) and did a Certificate in Employment and Training. Initially, he was at the bottom of the class. However, because he was not psychologically damaged, he worked hard and completed two years of work in one, and graduated with Certificate 2, and Certificate 3, of Skills for Work and Vocational Pathways. He also won a certificate of Outstanding Achievement. The next year he did a Diploma of Digital and Interactive Games, which enabled him to enter Western Sydney University. Currently, he is working through a Bachelor of Computer Science and is doing very well. Of all our children, Mark is the one who would have suffered the most in the school system. Sometimes I find it hard to believe this child, who was almost impossible to teach reading, writing, and simple arithmetic is competently dealing with long formulas, coding, and computer language. I thank God, that I was able to keep him at home and let him bloom at his own rate.

Marie our eldest, started a Bachelor of Arts at another University. She passed all her exams of the first semester, but due to the depravity incorporated in the content, she decided to drop the course. It is a decision we applaud. Instead, she writes and illustrates children's books. If you are interested, you can see a list of her books on Amazon under R.M. Hamilton.

Hannah went to Polytech at age seventeen and did a Foundations course for a year. She then went on to complete a Diploma in Multimedia. She now works for Qantas in Australia and regularly flies to Uganda to look after orphans in her holidays.

I am grateful to Raymond and Dorothy Moore for their thirty-year study on home-education. In the dark days, I clung to their prediction that home-schooling children often trail their peers until the late teens and then they rocket ahead and outstrip them. Truly, it has been this way for us.

Wendy Hamilton

About the Author

New Zealander Wendy Hamilton, was involved in homeschooling for over twenty years. She currently resides in Australia with her husband Ian and her four children. Wendy enjoys crafts, gardening, writing, and drawing.

Eating a Light Bulb does not make you Bright

Other Books By Wendy Hamilton

Darling the Window is on Fire

I told you not to Climb the Cactus.
Surviving the Badlands of Motherhood

Homemade Church

Children's Novels
The Britwhistles win a Prize
The Britwhistles and the Elasticizer

Children's Picture books
The Unlucky Snails
The Unlucky Snails go to France

These can be found at
www.zealauspublishing.com

www.ingramcontent.com/pod-product-compliance
Lightning Source LLC
Chambersburg PA
CBHW021103080526
44587CB00010B/355